*Routledge Revivals*

# Development, Experience and Curriculum in Primary Education

Originally published in 1984, this book considers the ever-increasing pressure that teachers are under both to demonstrate and maintain their professional understanding and competence. Curriculum development has long been the subject of scrutiny, with some authorities arguing that the primary curriculum should be a diluted version of the secondary curriculum. Professor Blyth presents a convincing case for a primary curriculum carefully constructed to enhance the relationship between the various aspects of the child's development and total experience.

Initially examining how children in the primary age range do develop and experience the world, the book goes on to consider the implications of this for shaping the curriculum. These are traced through different aspects of the primary curriculum, from physical, moral and aesthetic development to an understanding of the social world. The book concludes with an assessment of this approach to primary education within an international context and prospects for the future.

An important work by a leading authority, this book is a guide to the professional development of primary teachers, building on their experience and judgement.

# Development, Experience and Curriculum in Primary Education

W. A. L. Blyth

First published in 1984
by Croom Helm Ltd

This edition first published in 2018 by Routledge
2 Park Square, Milton Park, Abingdon, Oxon, OX14 4RN
and by Routledge
711 Third Avenue, New York, NY 10017

*Routledge is an imprint of the Taylor & Francis Group, an informa business*

© 1984 W. A. L. Blyth

All rights reserved. No part of this book may be reprinted or reproduced or utilised in any form or by any electronic, mechanical, or other means, now known or hereafter invented, including photocopying and recording, or in any information storage or retrieval system, without permission in writing from the publishers.

**Publisher's Note**
The publisher has gone to great lengths to ensure the quality of this reprint but points out that some imperfections in the original copies may be apparent.

**Disclaimer**
The publisher has made every effort to trace copyright holders and welcomes correspondence from those they have been unable to contact.

A Library of Congress record exists under LCCN: 84040036

ISBN 13: 978-1-138-55079-7 (hbk)
ISBN 13: 978-1-315-14735-2 (ebk)
ISBN 13: 978-1-138-55082-7 (pbk)

©1984 W.A.L. Blyth
Croom Helm Ltd, Provident House, Burrell Row,
Beckenham, Kent, BR3 1AT
Croom Helm Australia Pty Ltd, First Floor,
139 King Street, Sydney, NSW 2001, Australia

British Library Cataloguing in Publication Data

Blyth, W.A.L.
    Development, experience and curriculum in
    primary education. — (Croom Helm teaching 5–13
    series)
    1. Elementary schools — Curricula
    I. Title
    372.19     LB1570
    ISBN 0-7099-0641-2
    ISBN 0-7099-0642-0 Pbk

First published in the United States of America in 1984
All rights reserved. For information, write:
St. Martin's Press, Inc., 175 Fifth Avenue, New York, NY 10010

Library of Congress Card Catalog Number: 84-40036
ISBN 0-312-19686-5

# CONTENTS

List of Figures

Foreword

Acknowledgements

Preface

| | |
|---|---|
| 1. Development | 1 |
| 2. Experience | 14 |
| 3. Curriculum | 27 |
| 4. One Approach to Primary Education: an Enabling Curriculum | 41 |
| 5. Development, Experience and Aspects of the Formal Curriculum | 53 |
| 6. An Example: the Interpretation of the Social World | 80 |
| 7. Development, Experience and the Wider Curriculum | 99 |
| 8. Children's Response to the Primary Curriculum | 118 |
| 9. Teachers for an Enabling Curriculum | 134 |
| 10. An Enabling Curriculum in Perspective | 152 |
| Appendix I. An Enabling Curriculum for Primary Education | 168 |
| Appendix II. Examples of Autobiography and Fiction | 169 |
| Bibliography | 170 |
| Index | 175 |

# FIGURES

4.1 Static Relationship between Development, Experience and Curriculum    45

4.2 Dynamic Relationship between Development, Experience and Curriculum    46

**To the memory of my parents**

# FOREWORD

*Teaching 5—13* is a series of books intended to foster the professional development of teachers in primary and middle schools. The series is being published at a time when there are growing demands on teachers to demonstrate increasing levels of professional understanding and competence. Although the importance of personal qualities and social skills in successful teaching is acknowledged, the series is based on the premises that the enhancement of teacher competence and judgement in curricular and organisational matters is the major goal of pre-service and in-service teacher education and that this enhancement is furthered, not by the provision of recipes to be applied in any context, but by the application of practical principles for the organisation and management of learning and for the planning, implementation and evaluation of curricula. The series aims to help teachers and trainee teachers to think out for themselves ways of tackling the problems that confront them in their own particular range of circumstances. It does this by providing two kinds of books: those which focus on a particular area of the primary or middle school curriculum, and those which discuss general issues germane to any area of the curriculum.

Alan Blyth's book both respects and builds on primary teachers' judgement and competence and indicates how, in turn, teachers can enhance children's judgement and competence. It provides a rationale for primary education which not only avoids many of the tired arguments about child-centred and traditional education, but transcends them. Its basis is an original view of the curriculum—as planned intervention in the interaction between development and experience. The purpose of such a curriculum is general enablement: 'it is to equip the child not just with skills and content or even values and attitudes and understanding but with the capacity to choose and to accept and to cope'. The book itself enables; it provides a sense of direction and coherence to the enterprise of primary education. For those schools and individual teachers seeking a way forward in a post-Plowden, post-Black Paper era, it presents a challenging argument; for those interested in any one of the many facets of children's school experience, it provides valuable insights.

THE SERIES EDITOR

# ACKNOWLEDGEMENTS

It would be impossible to list all those who have contributed, directly or indirectly, to the making of this book. Ideas usually have more origins than we realise. However, I am particularly grateful to Dr Philomena Alston, of Chester College of Higher Education, who drew my attention to the relevance of her own research to the question of musical development; to Mr Peter Kennerley, of the Faculty of Education, Liverpool Polytechnic, whose expertise in children's literature proved of great assistance in the preparation of Chapter 8; to Mr John Vaughan, Tutor Librarian to the School of Education, University of Liverpool, for his incredible patience in answering all enquiries ranging from the rudimentary to the obscure; and to all, especially in my own family, who have endured the labour involved in writing it. I should also like to thank Mrs Felicity Jones and Mrs Norma Prout for the cheerful and efficient way in which they deciphered my manuscript and typed the book.

# PREFACE

Recently the primary curriculum has become the subject of considerable attention. There are many reasons why this should be so, the most obvious being the extent to which public scrutiny is now focused on what is a major arena of public expenditure, as well as a major producer of human resources, throughout the world.

This book is planned as an extended essay, intended to make one contribution to the continuing debate on the primary curriculum. It has no pretensions to being a major treatise, nor even an academic monograph embodying extensive research or analysis on any one aspect of the curriculum. Nor, on the other hand, does it purport to lay down a curriculum that a school could adopt, adapt, or implement in detail. There are some loose ends in the argument, and many conceptual and empirical defects; but a wide range of ideas is considered. What the book attempts to do is to draw together and formulate a point of view within the general debate, one which individual teachers can continue to think about when designing their own curriculum, if they may, and in adapting an official curriculum, if they must.

There is also another, rather different, reason why this book cannot be regarded as a detailed map of a curriculum. No one author could presume to write in the same detail, and with the same degree of justification, about the primary curriculum as a whole. Almost always, one aspect will be more familiar than another, and more in accordance with an author's expertise. Of course, primary teachers are expected to handle the curriculum as a whole, and that alone entitles them to much admiration and support; but that is a different matter from claiming to speak about all of it with the same degree of authority.

Another necessary limitation in any author's equipment is that it is likely to be derived from one, or two, national systems more fully than from any others. In my case, I am much more familiar with England and Wales, and in particular with certain widely scattered parts of England, than with any other context of primary education. Even Scotland is distinctly less familiar to me, although I do have a nodding acquaintance with some overseas systems. However, I have tried to write about primary education as a world phenomenon, with an emphasis on the years 6 to 12, though it will probably be evident that I am used to reading about English primary education and also thinking in terms of the English system with its entry age (for compulsory education) of 5, its usual break at about 7 when children move from infant to junior schools, and its conclusion at 11, with modifications of the transfer ages to 8 and 12, or 9 and 13, in the areas in which middle schools have been established (Blyth and Derricott, 1977; Hargreaves and Tickle, 1980). Within this age-span, more attention has been paid to the older than to the younger years, simply because the curriculum becomes more complex and differentiated as children grow older.

The theme of the book is the need to consider the primary curriculum in relation to children's development and experience as a whole. There is nothing strikingly novel in this. What I have aimed to do is to think a little further about the way in which development and experience interact, inside and outside formal education, and how the curriculum can relate actively to both. This has led me to take up a position a little different from what is usually termed 'progressive' or 'child-centred', though it has much in common with what those terms imply. The difference is that the claims of forms of understanding are also substantially taken into account. The outcome of the discussion is that a case is put forward for an *enabling curriculum*.

The first four chapters take the argument to this point. One long chapter, the fifth, covers the formal curriculum as a whole, and then Chapter 6 indicates how one aspect of curriculum, the understanding of the social world, which is my particular interest, can be developed in greater detail. Chapter 7 completes this exposition with a consideration of the wider curriculum: informal, organisational and hidden. In Chapter 8 an attempt is made to examine how children themselves may respond to curriculum, and what this implies for an enabling approach. Chapter 9 considers what such a curricular stance involves for teachers, their roles and their professional development. Finally, in Chapter 10, primary education is viewed in a wider context in place and time, and some attempt is made to appraise the value of an enabling curriculum in the real world of today and tomorrow. The whole argument of the book is summarised in Appendix I.

One significant topic has been deliberately excluded from the main discussion. No reference is made to the specific ways in which an enabling curriculum can be worked out in schools for children with special educational needs. This is not because they are relatively few, at least in the more prosperous parts of the world, or because doubts have been cast on the value of separate provision, but simply because the treatment that could have been given to this topic within the scope of the present volume would have been rather perfunctory and therefore misleading. However, some reference to children with handicaps is made in Chapter 8.

Sometimes I marvel that teachers in primary schools show so much patience, understanding and sheer endurance. Perhaps one reason for this professional triumph is to be found in the personal satisfaction, evident in primary education at least in the more affluent countries, that comes from watching the development and experience of children that takes place before their eyes. For some teachers, there will also be a motivation derived from a system of belief, and I think that for them, and in particular for those who are Christians, an enabling curriculum will have a deeper significance. For all teachers, I hope that the discussion of ideas in this book may help to illuminate the primary curriculum, and that in the process they may go a little further in the construction of their own experience and professional development.

Alan Blyth
University of Liverpool

# 1 DEVELOPMENT

Development is a term that is used in a number of ways. It is possible to develop an argument, or a disease, or a film, or a policy. One way of describing the Third World is that it consists of 'developing countries'. Each of these uses of the term carries with it a set of overtones and images, which together surround the notion of 'development'. All of them do, however, imply some kind of programmed, purposive change.

One kind of development has acquired a distinctiveness of its own: it is the kind that is associated with organisms. They develop through an in-built programme which, however much it may be modified through external influences, depends essentially on a genetically determined inheritance. This is true whether the organism is a wasp or a seaweed or a kangaroo. Only over long periods do evolutionary processes noticeably affect a species. For an individual organism the direction of development is predictable and intransitive. The individual does not develop something; it just develops, purposefully and evidently.

Yet the term 'development' is not usually applied to kangaroos or seaweeds or wasps; it is in practice reserved for one particular organism, the human one. Child Development, as a field of study, is now a century old and has been given a high measure of academic standing over the years by seminal writers such as Arnold Gesell and Susan Isaacs.[1] Usually it considers various aspects of physical growth together with the formation of intellect and personality, taking account also of the various social and environmental influences that affect these aspects of development. Normally, a set of four aspects—physical, cognitive, emotional, social—or something similar is taken as the framework within which child development is discussed, although Peters (1969, p.5) and Alexander (forthcoming) have indicated that the interaction of these conventional categories may be more complex than is sometimes assumed. Together they constitute a major topic in human biology and psychology and indeed in wider fields including sociology, philosophy and theology, for they are concerned with theories, and evidence, about what nature is, and what human nature is. Moreover, they carry with them implications about the responsibilities that adults, especially parents and teachers, must adopt towards children. Although no one set of attitudes and responses can cover all interpretations of nature and of human nature, there is no escaping the imperative to formulate some principles on which to act. Thus Child Development, however its study may be organised, presents a practical challenge to any educator.

The first subdivision usually singled out for study in this field is *physical development.* This one is the most readily linked to the programmed unfolding of the organism. Skeletal, muscular and glandular development all take place in ways that resemble the development of other immature organisms. The process of development itself includes mere increase in size: this aspect is growth. It also includes the attainment of new powers such as those of sexual reproduction; this aspect is maturation. Both aspects of development proceed according to a programme that is genetically determined, proceeding by spurts and curves that are similar for all individuals but in absolute detail unique for each individual. Incidentally, we are more aware than formerly of the extent to which sexual development takes place during childhood as well as during adolescence. The actual onset of puberty itself occurs earlier than in, say, Victorian times—Tanner's (1961) 'secular trend'—so that, at least for girls, it is more likely to fall within the bounds of primary education.

Although the programme is unique for each individual, its actual implementation is not entirely predictable. It depends in part on those social and environmental influences that have already been mentioned. External circumstances, such as accident, or privation of stimulus or nourishment, exercise various kinds of constraints, and this is a lifelong process.

There is still one other element in physical development to be considered, and that is the active response of the organism to its environment that we call learning. Even in this physical sphere there is ample evidence that growth and maturation are immensely overlain by the outcomes of learning. Yet however much they are overlain, they cannot be discarded or ignored.

Physical development is the aspect of development in which children most evidently resemble other immature organisms. It is also the aspect which is most readily open to observation, not only by others but by children themselves. The other aspects of development, as we shall see, largely conceal their own future from children. It is not really possible for a child, however intelligent or socially competent or morally precocious, to imagine what he or she will be like as an adult, because the capacity to understand the direction of those aspects of development depends on processes which are themselves part of development. But it is quite possible for children to envisage being bigger and stronger and more agile and more good-looking, since these categories of growth are understood by children from their earliest years. Only in respect of sexual drives is this basis of personal knowledge largely lacking before adolescence. Therefore it is not surprising that children tend to regard development largely *as* physical development, and to stress to themselves and others the significance of physical feats and competences, with important consequences for other aspects of development, as Tanner (1961) and others have emphasised.

The second principal aspect of development usually singled out, at least for descriptive purposes, is *intellectual development*. It can be envisaged as an extension of physical development into a realm that is almost peculiar to human beings. For here, too, it is possible to speak of the growth of mental powers, and of the maturation of particular capacities, and most certainly of learning, for this is the aspect of development which is concerned with the capacity to learn, self-consciously, and through tasks matched to intellectual growth, the element on which Margaret Donaldson (1978) lays particular emphasis. However, it differs from physical development in one obvious but critical way. Most physical development is open to inspection: that is why children can understand its significance. Intellectual development is not. There is of course a crude relationship between the size and shape of the brain and the intellectual capacity of the organism, but this applies only in the most general terms in the evolutionary scale. Where individuals are concerned, intellectual development cannot be seen. It can only be inferred from observed behaviour. This year Julie is taller than last year, and she can use a calculator. But whereas she is invariably taller, she sometimes uses the calculator the right way and sometimes the wrong way, and sometimes she doesn't want to use it at all. Soon, use of the calculator may become, in a significant phrase, 'second nature' to her, but for the time being it is difficult to point to what has changed since last year. What is more, to Julie herself it is evident that she can sometimes use the calculator, but not that she has undergone some kind of general development, whereas she can see that she can run and also jump and again, swim better because her whole physical potential has become greater.

This invisibility of intellectual development is accompanied by a greater range of theoretical explanations than in the case of physical development, at least in modern times. In the preceding paragraph it was suggested that intellectual development can be envisaged as an extension of physical development. It is also possible to envisage it as something entirely different. Indeed, the history of philosophy and of psychology during the past 200 years shows some of the controversies that have surrounded this particular issue. For it is at least possible to regard intellectual development as having very little to do with the kind of genetic programming that influences physical development. If there is a soul, or a mind, which is not entirely a function of the physical organism, then its development may follow a quite different pattern. It may even be complete from the start and not liable to development at all; requiring only interaction with the environment to bring it into play. Even if it does require development, that could be the result entirely of a learning process and not at all of something genetically determined. Although it is nowadays customary, at least, to assume that intellectual development is related to physical development, it is necessary to remember that this is not self-evident.

The evidence in favour of regarding intellectual development as similar to physical development is, of course, derived from observation and experiment. The early work of Sully, Preyer and Stanley Hall[2] has been followed by that of many others and in particular of Piaget and his followers[3]. Together they have accumulated an impressive mass of evidence in favour of the view that there is a sequence of intellectual development that is broadly similar for all children. Although any one set of views about intellectual development is—rightly—liable to constant criticism and revaluation, the case for the general assumption that intellectual powers develop much as physical powers do remains a strong one. It has in fact given rise to a whole discipline named 'genetic psychology' or 'developmental psychology' whose findings are widely accepted. Indeed, there is some danger that they may be too directly and mechanically transferred from one situation to another, on the assumption that the details of intellectual development are much more uniform than they necessarily are. For the establishment of a general principle does not eliminate the need for the cautious, detailed working out of its applications. Experiments with jars or marbles may give little guidance for the understanding of social relations.

The strengths and limitations of the genetic approach can be illustrated by referring to stages of intellectual development such as those that Piaget identified. Like Whitehead before him and Bruner after him[4], Piaget denoted modes of operation which constituted a hierarchy. Starting from pre-operational thinking, he identified what are usually defined as a phase of intuitive reasoning, then a phase of concrete operations, involving trying out hypotheses to solve problems, and finally a phase of propositional thinking in which more than one hypothesis can be handled at one and the same time. He saw the individual as ascending this hierarchy by a progressive set of adjustments (assimilation and accommodation) and of 'de-centering' or the progressive transcending of an egocentric interpretation of the world. This enormous contribution to the understanding of intellectual development has an obvious significance for all planned learning. Yet it was not intended to depict a unitary process of development. It might apply at an early stage in life to one kind of learning, and later to another. For the same reason it could be only broadly linked with chronological age. Just as in physical development individuals move differently, so also this is still more true of intellectual development. Piaget was concerned with the understanding of a set of processes; he never claimed to have drawn up a universal, chronological map.

The remaining aspects of development, as usually depicted, may be considered together, though logically they are distinct. These are *personality development* (or emotional development) and *social development*. Personality development is the more inclusive term, covering various kinds of purposive and emotional behaviour, while social development refers more specifically to interaction in social situations. Yet the two are linked, because there are few aspects of personality that can be detected otherwise than in social interaction.

All the uncertainties that apply to intellectual development apply at least as markedly to personal/social development. They, too, can only be inferred from observed behaviour. They, too, can be regarded as dependent on the same kind of genetic programme as physical development; or alternatively, they may be looked upon as almost entirely the consequence of learning. Moreover, whereas the weight of evidence about intellectual development is in favour of the genetic interpretation, however much it is open to environmental modification, there is no such agreement about personal/social development.

There is not even agreement about the nature of the genetic interpretation itself. One genetic view is that personal/social interaction becomes richer and more complex as the organism develops, just as in the case of physical development. But alongside this there is the rather different view derived from psychoanalysis. That view also permits of stages, like the Piagetian stages of intellectual development, but it also depends on assumptions about the unconscious mind that are derived from the clinical work of Sigmund Freud and his followers and from others in a similar tradition[5]. These assumptions are even less open to observation and verification than those that are usually made about the intellect; in fact, they are virtually metaphysical in nature, though evidently useful in interpreting some kinds of mental disturbance. However, by claiming that a kind of sexuality is characteristic of the early years, to be followed by a period of 'latency' and a sexual revival in adolescence, they have sometimes appeared to set up a model of development that is discontinuous and thus incompatible with the description of progressive development that is now generally accepted in the physical and intellectual spheres.

The ideas of those who take a different genetic view of personal/social development show, in this field, a fairly close parallel with the generally accepted sequence in intellectual development. Piaget himself has contributed substantially to this field too[6], and his work has been importantly extended by others such as Kohlberg. Stages have been postulated in moral development: in fact, in social development with a component of moral understanding and imperative. Specific attention will be paid to this issue in Chapter 5, but in a general consideration of development it is noteworthy that the same advantages and limitations apply here as in the case of intellectual development. On the one hand it is important to explore the justification for saying that there are recognisable stages in social development. On the other hand it is essential to remember that there is no one rigid chronological sequence that can be applied to every individual or group. Meanwhile, other theories have been developed from insights into anthropology and social psychology by influential writers with very different emphases such as Erikson (1950) and Havighurst (1953), both of whom have been more concerned with a sequence of social orientations and competences than with specifically moral development. Together, these theories have provided a stimulus for much research and for at least some policies relating to the place of childhood and youth in society.

Meanwhile there is also disagreement among those who regard personal/social development as something learned rather than genetically determined. It is here that ideological considerations tend to arise. A Marxist view is bound to give primacy to one major set of social circumstances, the ownership of the means of production, as the major determinant of these aspects of development. It is, however, also possible to emphasise the decisive importance of family and small-group contexts in the development of particular individuals, as do those with an interactionist perspective. Thus, both the genetic and the environmental approaches are themselves subdivided, though there remains between these two major approaches one clear distinction. The former places emphasis on innate characteristics; the latter does not.

Any brief summary of this kind must do scant justice to the range and subtlety of the issues involved, but it may serve to indicate the nature of the uncertainties surrounding any theories of child development. For it is illegitimate to approach problems of education and teaching without at least some consideration of these issues.

**Some Development Approaches to Primary Education**

Part of the legacy of educational thought which permeates current thinking is derived from writers and thinkers who have, for one reason or another, based their approach to education on developmental considerations. In order to understand the present situation more fully it will be helpful to turn next to a brief examination of some of their views, which are still influential.

Before any of these is considered in detail, it is important to remember the obvious point that child development is a process that continues throughout life, whereas formal education is a limited, temporary, intermittent procedure. Development can take place without formal education, as indeed it has done in pre-literate societies. But formal education cannot take place without the adoption of some stance towards development.

The earliest references to development in writings about education were formulated in an intellectual climate very different from our own. In ancient and medieval times in the West, and during the Renaissance, educational aims were largely focused upon notions of excellence that were derived from ideals of perfection rather than from processes of development: Plato's *Republic* was their most illustrious embodiment. However intelligent, humane and adaptable the procedures of formal education were, they remained associated with a view of human nature which regarded developing children as in some way inadequate, so that the wind of intellectual and moral stimulation had regrettably to be tempered to them until the significant part of life was reached. As Ariès and others have shown[7], it was not until about the seventeenth century that childhood was generally recognised as a positive phase of life. Previously the more humane writers had done little more than plead for more recognition of children's inability to learn to embark at a tender age on the essentials of a literary curriculum.

During the seventeenth century, however, some writers began to think more purposefully about children's development. As they extended their attention from the study of letters to the study of Nature, they became more aware of human nature, and of child Nature, as a part of nature, and began to recommend different approaches for different age-levels. The greatest of them all, Comenius, stands intriguingly at the point of division between two ages, being concerned still with classical traditions and ideals, yet also reaching out towards a scientific culture and some form of universal educational provision. It is characteristic of his stance that he called for the adjustment of formal education to stages of development, but that when he came to demarcate those stages he assigned equal age-spans to each of them, and decided that each was appropriate for one of the major steps in an educative programme based not on development, but on what he regarded as the logic of his curriculum[8].

It was, however, during the eighteenth century that for the first time educational theories emerged which were actually based on developmental principles. The rationalism of the early Enlightenment did little to stimulate this, for Enlightenment Man wished to make as few concessions as Renaissance Man had done to the weaknesses and foibles of childhood. But as the eighteenth century progressed, there appeared within the general framework of the Enlightenment itself a new Romantic strain, which laid less emphasis on Reason and more on feeling; which emphasised, in fact, the whole of human nature, and which came to share with the earlier rationalism only a common opposition to the traditions and dogmas of the past. As Bantock (1980) suggests, the emphasis moved from improving on Nature ('artifice') to following Nature herself. And the writer associated indelibly with this movement was Jean-Jacques Rousseau.

It was Rousseau's principal claim to originality as a thinker on education that he was the first writer who in *Emile*[9] not only described formal education in developmental terms, but who also derived his stages of development from the observation of child nature itself instead of from the content of education. The fact that Rousseau was not a very good or a very accurate observer of child nature, and that the education that he proposed as a response to the stages he observed was at best tentative and at worst preposterous, in no way detracts from the originality of this one central idea. For the first time it was seriously considered that children's development might be a guide rather than a limitation to the educational process itself.

Rousseau's successors in the later eighteenth and early nineteenth centuries adapted and modified, and qualified, his approach. Basedow, Pestalozzi and Fellenberg were among those whose work attracted widespread attention. Pestalozzi in particular came to enunciate the dependence of the development of knowledge on the prior development of feeling, and also to acknowledge that experience (our next theme) should improve on development as embodied in 'blind' nature[10]. Meanwhile, revolutions in North America and then in France and elsewhere in Europe led to widespread questioning of the older bases for education, while the Romantic movement in literature presented childhood in a new guise. Wordsworth's *Prelude* is the best-known embodiment of this new attitude, presenting early childhood as both important and innocent, but others such as Blake contributed to it. In that cultural climate a new way of organising education was certain of a hearing, and the developmental principle proved particularly appealing.

It was Pestalozzi's follower and critic Froebel who was responsible for the next major modification in the developmental approach. He was almost the first to present the process of education as the tending of children as though they were plants. The famous 'plant metaphor' was thus particularly his, and the term 'kindergarten' he regarded as revealed to him almost in a moment of divine inspiration[11]. Indeed, there was an element of mysticism and almost of religious awe in the way in which he approached the education of children itself. He did not just observe stages of development. He took it for granted that development was programmed and that education consisted of the planned interaction of that programmed development with the external world or, as he put it, 'making the inner outer and the outer, inner'.[12] In the course of elaborating this notion, Froebel too seems sometimes to have allowed his vision to run away with his grasp of reality, but he continued to be involved with actual schools and with teacher training throughout his life, so that he was never as separated from the educative process as Rousseau had been.

He also elaborated the notion of programmed development in one important way, by stressing the importance of 'budding points' in each child's life, which were the moments at which particular powers such as a capacity for language or number could best be harnessed and extended. To try to do so earlier would be premature; to delay too long would be to miss the best opportunity.

Further developmental approaches to education have been evolved during the present century. Montessori, though in her turn critical of Froebel, in fact adopted many of his ideas, but based them much more firmly on the observation proper to a trained medical expert. It is interesting that she preferred the term 'sensitive periods' to that of 'budding points', choosing as it were a neurological rather than a horticultural figure of speech[13]. Montessori did in fact engage in prolonged and systematic observation of children, evolving eventually a coherent theory about which she became rather imperiously possessive, but it is one which still has considerable relevance and a considerable following. Meanwhile, others such as Rudolf Steiner (1969) have taken the stages of physical growth, in particular, and have erected around them a whole philosophy of development. Indeed, a whole developmental tradition[14] acquired cohesion and distinctiveness after the First World War. This tradition underwent a further distinct modification, in some of its manifestations, under the influence of Freud and other psychoanalytic writers, who emphasised the inescapable biological imperative of sexual development throughout childhood and adolescence, a claim that horrified some of their contemporaries, but left a strong impression on others, including the young A. S. Neill (Croall, 1983).

In retrospect these writers have left an important legacy of thinking about the educative process in relation to child development, one which for two reasons cannot be disregarded. The first reason is that they are part and parcel of the matrix of thought within which we all operate. Education, like any other intellectual enterprise, has its own founding fathers (and mothers). The other is that their thinking is still regarded in many quarters as valid for our own time.

In discussions of primary education these developmental writers are particularly important for what may appear to be a rather pedestrian reason. Having sketched the course of children's development, they tended to try to map it in detail, starting with the youngest age-group. This enterprise absorbed so much of their interest and effort that their own lifetimes did not prove long enough to devote an equivalent amount of attention to each other age-group. Thus, Froebel wrote only the first book of the *Education of Man*, and Montessori's writings about adolescence were sketchy and unsystematic when compared with what she had to say about the education of younger children. The probably unintended outcome of this maldistribution of their writings has been that developmental theorists seem to have had much more to say about primary than about secondary education, and to have said it much better. The impression may have been given that they were not interested in anything beyond childhood, or even that their theories could only apply to childhood. That is not true: there are many individual references in their writings which indicate the potential scope of their own constructs. Nevertheless, they have made their principal contribution at the primary stage, and have ensured that here, at least, developmental considerations must be taken into account.

The decline of systematic developmental thinking about primary education has deprived us of some sense of co-ordinated purpose, even if it has been associated with a desirable growth of critical awareness. But that decline is not complete. There are writers who still dare to present a consistent theoretical approach.

One of these is Kieran Egan (1979), whose work *Educational Development* represents a systematic attempt to propose an educational policy that takes into account the developmental considerations already discussed. His strikingly unusual contribution to the whole question of development is one that takes account of the various contributions from psychology and other social sciences, but is, as its title indicates, essentially a scheme for educational development. In this he is firmly in the tradition of writers on education such as Rousseau and Froebel and also of Whitehead, whose work he explicitly recognises as similar. Like Montessori, he also uses the concept of sensitive periods. Unlike some of the earlier writers, he does not confine himself to the earlier years, but prescribes an approach to education up to full adulthood. As with any other closely reasoned and important book, it is quite impossible to do justice to its arguments in a brief summary, but something of the flavour of Egan's approach can be inferred from the titles of the four stages which he postulates: mythic, romantic, philosophic, ironic. Of these, only the first and part of the second are assigned approximately to the age-span of primary education. Nevertheless, he has given us something positive to discuss. It would be welcome if others could offer such stimulating original contributions as this on the significance of educational development.

Egan emphasises the characteristic feature of educational development, namely that it is concerned with the *content* of the educative process, whereas other theories of development tend to be concerned with the constraints that set bounds to that process. Like other writers before him he is concerned with the interaction between development and a curriculum adapted to development. Few thinkers concerned with development in relation to education have adopted any fundamentally different position. For development may be seen as a necessary major element in the planning of education. Further, it may confer a sequence on the process of education through progression from the less to the more 'developed state', as Kohlberg and Mayer (1972) term it. It may even be seen as providing some of the data of education itself, when children reflect on their physical or social or moral behaviour, and when, as can often be seen, they perceive the next stage in their own development and strive to think and act in accordance with it (Kohlberg and Mayer, 1972, p. 483). But it cannot fully determine the pattern of education. To attempt to derive the curriculum itself from developmental considerations would virtually deny any directive role to education. It would imply a kindergarten without fertilisers; without tools, even without a gardener. As Peters (1969, p. 8) suggested, it might be easier to envisage development as dependent on education than to think of education as dependent on development. The most that developmental theory can claim to do is to set the bounds of curriculum, and to suggest some of its tasks.

Development is not, however, the only process that can make a contribution of this kind. The next chapter considers the claims of Experience.

**Notes**

1. Arnold Gesell and his associates developed profiles of individual children's growth and development, and from these established a series of descriptions of average children at different age-levels (Gesell, 1948). Susan Isaacs evolved her approach to child development largely through her experience at the Malting House School in Cambridge, and subsequently initiated the Department of Child Develop-

ment of the University of London Institute of Education. For a general survey of her views see Isaacs (1948).

2. James Sully and W. Preyer carried out close observational studies in Europe. G. Stanley Hall was one of the most influential pioneers of child development studies in the United States: his most important work was in the field of adolescence.

3. Jean Piaget's work, which has been more influential than any other in recent years in respect of children's cognitive development, was initially concerned more with logic and epistemology than with the established aspects of cognitive psychology. Jerome Bruner is perhaps his most eminent reinterpreter. There is a wealth of writing by, and on, both.

4. Whitehead's three 'ages' were designated as: romance, precision, and generalisation (Whitehead, 1932). Of these, the first was regarded as coinciding broadly with the primary years, though minor 'cycles' of the same three phases could develop at any time as new interests emerged. Bruner's triad embraces three 'forms of representation': enactive, iconic and symbolic (Bruner, 1966, Ch. 1).

5. The literature of psychoanalysis is voluminous, but it may be broadly grouped into those writers who followed and interpreted Freud's own approach, and those who adopted the somewhat different emphases of Carl Jung and of Alfred Adler. All three groups emphasised the prime importance of the subconscious elements of mind.

6. Piaget's main contribution in this sphere is through his experiments on moral judgement (Piaget, 1932). Lawrence Kohlberg, whose work is mentioned in Chapter 5, has been his most significant disciple in this respect.

7. There is now a substantial literature on the history of childhood, including the writings of Ariès (1962), de Mause (1974), and Sommerville (1982). Musgrove (1964) has also contributed to the same general theme. Further reference is made to this topic in Chapter 10.

8. In *The Great Didactic* (1657), tr. M.W. Keatinge (A. and C. Black, 1896).

9. J-J. Rousseau, *Emile* (1762), tr. B. Foxley (Everyman Library, 1911).

10. This view is embodied in Pestalozzi's *How Gertrude Teaches Her Children* (1801), tr. L.E. Holland and F.C. Turner (Swann Sonnenschein, 1894).

11. This is Froebel's claim in his autobiography, tr. E. Michaelis and E.K. Moore (Allen & Unwin, 1896).

12. See his *Education of Man* (1826). tr. W.N. Hailmann, (Appleton, 1897).

13. In particular in *Il Metodo della Pedagogia Scientifica* (1912), tr. A.E. George as *The Montessori Method* (Heinemann, 1912).

14. Its characteristics are indicated in standard histories of education and of educational thought as well as in contemporary accounts. The term 'developmental tradition' as applied to English primary education was introduced into an earlier study of my own (Blyth, 1965, vol. 2), and although perhaps it was given a rather too broad connotation, I think it is still a meaningful description of an important part of thinking about English primary education that does not derive from the 'elemenatary' or 'preparatory' elements in its ancestry.

# 2 EXPERIENCE

Like some other aspects of mental life, such as interest, experience has two aspects. It involves both the subjective act of experiencing and the objective, the thing experienced (Oakeshott, 1933). Of the two the subjective is the more important, since it is the one that forms a part of the mind in action and in growth; and the more general the concept of experience becomes, the more prominent the subjective element in it is seen to be. It is in the light of this binary nature of experience that its educational significance can be explored.

The term 'experience', with this binary quality, is used in several distinct ways. At the most discrete level it refers to particular occurrences which are described as experiences. It is an experience to stub one's toe, or to meet an old friend unexpectedly, or to see a snowscape, or hear a famous orchestra. It can hardly be said that all of these discrete experiences are equal in quality or importance, but the term 'experience' is applicable to all of them, and all of them have a subjective as well as an objective component.

A second meaning of the term refers to the sum of all these particular events. It is in this sense that we refer to an individual's 'experience' as a whole, or to a substantial part of it, as when an applicant for a post is asked to state 'qualifications and experience'. At this level the subjective component is more prominent, for it is the common feature linking the aggregate together.

A third sense of the term, perhaps less immediately relevant to the present discussion but educationally significant none the less, has overtones of acquired competence. An 'experienced' traveller is not just one who has travelled on countless planes and trains without ever learning to manage his tickets and currency and baggage. It is assumed that he or she has become more capable as a result of these travels, to the point of being able to advise others. In this third use of the term 'experience', the subjective element alone is present.

There is also a fourth sense in which 'experience' is used: as a technical term in philosophy or psychology. It implies, as it were, all the other uses in a bracket. When we speak of 'intelligence' or 'cognition', we have a technical or semi-technical term available to cover the category, but in the case of 'experience' we use the same term to describe the category, the concept, of experience, as we do for the actual acts or sequences of experience.

In the following discussion the emphasis will be on the second of these four uses, namely how an individual's total experience can affect what he is and what he may become, though all four are to some extent relevant to the theme. Of course, philosophers would wish to undertake a much fuller analysis of the term, but this introduction will at least serve to indicate the sort of issue that is raised by the use of this word 'experience', which has figured so extensively in writings of so many kinds throughout the ages.

Prominent among these writings has been a point of view about learning and about knowledge. This assumes that the learner or knower is independent from what is learned or known until some interaction occurs through which learning takes place. In other words the subjective and objective components of experience are seen as distinct until this interaction takes place. In the case of one of the instances already mentioned, the man who sees the snowscape is there before he meets the snowscape, and so is the snowscape; but the experience takes place when, and only when, they meet. How that learning, that interaction, takes place depends on particular assumptions about minds and perceptions and brains.

It is possible for a theory of experience to be entirely compatible with a theory of development. For any theory of development allows for some kind of interaction between the organism and the environment, and this interaction is experience. On the other hand it is also possible for a theory of experience to be at least partly independent of any theory of development.

In the purely physical domain, this is manifestly absurd because there, development is so palpable. The most that experience can do is to influence physical development by means of exercise and practice. It is meaningful to describe a man as an experienced swimmer, and at the same to say that he has developed from a boy champion to an adult champion. It would be absurd to expect him to be an adult champion while he is still a boy.

However, in the less visible intellectual and personal/social domains the role of experience can be regarded as quite genuinely separate from much that is normally considered as development. In the case of intellectual powers the role of experience was initially asserted as against one particular developmental view, namely the assumption that ideas and concepts were inborn. From Plato to St Augustine and some of the Renaissance thinkers, and even to

Descartes and his followers, the mind was looked upon as in some way stocked with powers and ideas that required only to be sensitised, unfolded or exercised. Of course, this assumption could not be proved, nor disproved. For that reason it permitted an alternative and equally unprovable assumption, namely that the mind began life with no stock of ideas or concepts at all, but only with the power to acquire them. In that case experience must have a much more decisive part to play. Instead of interacting with development in the production of ideas, it is itself directly responsible for their existence. Instead of merely shaping ideas, it gives birth to them. The objective element in experience thus acquires a more prominent position. This view, with its emphasis on the senses as the source of knowledge, can be detected in different forms when Aristotle is compared with Plato, St Thomas Aquinas with St Augustine, or Locke with Descartes. It is from this kind of assumption that the empirical tradition in philosophy, with its many subtleties and variations, has evolved, with its emphasis on a theory of knowledge dependent on the correspondence of mental constructs with sense perceptions, rather than on the intrinsic coherence and perfection of ideas as a criterion of truth. This empirical tradition may of course itself be challenged in turn by other interpretations of experience, such as those derived from phenomenology, which maintain that forms of mental activity must be developed prior to experience, even if that claim cannot be made for ideas themselves[1].

At first sight these issues may appear somewhat pretentious if viewed as a consequence of anything so apparently straightforward and embedded in commonsense language as 'learning through experience'; yet it is the case that they do arise from this everyday context. As in so many other matters, it is impossible to interpret what is going on in a home or a playgroup or a classroom without making assumptions about such basic questions.

Much the same is true if we turn to the question of personal/social experience. As in the case of intellectual competence, it is possible to look upon experience as little more than the area of interaction between an in-built personality and its social environment. But again, as with intellectual competence, it is also possible to regard personal/social qualities as largely, even almost entirely, derived from outside the individual. In that case experience is again independent of development, and all aspects of personality and of social behaviour are derived from it.

Thus, it is possible to assert, though not to prove, that experience is an important independent element in children's lives. Instead of being like plants with built-in growth patterns or toys with built-in programmes, they appear more like video-cameras, recording what they see and hear, and building up a store of tapes from which to make selections and combinations and interpretations. Of course, if the analogy, or even the assumption, is pushed too far, difficulties arise. The phenomenologists raise an objection at this point also, wondering how far it is legitimate to say that the video-cameras embody their own intentions in recording, rather than simply being pointed at phenomena and mirroring what they happen to pick up. Just as development cannot be absolute, ignoring the environment altogether, so experience cannot be absolute even in intellectual and personal/social affairs, ignoring the means of learning and knowing altogether. There is an innate component, and there are external stimuli. The argument is about their relative importance and independence, and about the nature of the interaction between them that, on any definition, constitutes experience.

Having considered some of the general issues relating to the role of experience in human affairs, we may now take a closer look at their significance for education, and in particular, examine certain characteristics of experience which are particularly central to educational concerns.

The first consideration among these is one that has always interested philosophers and psychologists. It refers to the way in which experience is gained, and the implications which this has for education. Because of its sensory basis, the acquisition of experience must depend partly on development. The nature of experience is for the newly born that 'big, booming, buzzing confusion' of which William James spoke, and it is only with the fuller development of the sense organs that experience can be analysed and thus made meaningful. It therefore follows that any individual with sensory deficiency will also have a different set of experiences from another with full sensory equipment, though this does not mean that these experiences are necessarily inferior in quality: witness the achievements of the blind. It could also be claimed that any individual with innate intellectual deficiency will have a different set of experiences from those that are, statistically, normal, though here too questions of quality are much more problematic.

It is important to realise that this dependence on the senses does not in itself affect the claim of experience to be independent of development. Even if the acquisition of knowledge and ideas is dependent on sensory capacities, that does not mean that the knowledge and ideas are themselves an outcome of sensory development. The actual contents of the mind may still be unpredictable and entirely the result of what experiences the individual actually has.

It is also necessary to remember, as Dearden (1968) emphasises, that experience does not just happen. It must be based on percepts that themselves depend on cognitive powers and often on taught procedures. To use the earlier analogy, the video-cameras do not roam randomly, but come to be programmed to record in a purposive, trained manner. Thus, in a sense, experience depends on learning just as much as learning depends on experience. It is the interaction between the two, the disciplined relationship between the subjective and the objective components, that expands horizons.

What is more, each individual does, to some extent, construct his or her own experience. Unlike development, with its programmed characteristics, experience is both unpredictable and also dependent upon some element of choice. Whatever may be true of each specific experience, the sequence of experiences include some examples which have been chosen instead of others; some journeys, some companions, some clothes and so forth. Within formal education much the same is true. Sometimes the choice is permitted, or encouraged. Even when it is not, there remains the choice about how far to enter into what is offered as education or whether to enter into it at all. To this extent each individual has some control over what enters into experience. To this extent each individual makes his own world.

The second of these characteristics of experience is that, like development, it is continuous. That does not mean that it is unbroken. Sleep, amnesia, and the impossibility of attending to every stimulus simultaneously, all point to the fragmented and arbitrary way in which the sequence of experience is constructed. None the less, it is generally continuous and cumulative. Past experience is the basis of present experience; and when in old age this relation of past to present is dislocated, intellectual and personal/social powers are dislocated too. Death could even be regarded as the final detachment of present experience from past experience. So this continuity of experience implies that earlier experiences are partially indelible. Therapy can reduce, but cannot eliminate, the effects of intellectual or social misfortune or deprivation.

The third characteristic of experience arises from the first. This is that experience is *total*. No institutional context, whether family, school, community or nation can substantiate a claim to take part of experience and make it the whole. This rather obvious, but often overlooked, truth is particularly well illustrated in novels and autobiographies.

A fourth characteristic of experience that may at first sight appear to contradict the second and third is that it varies in quality and intensity. It is quite usual for people to say that one particular experience, within the stream of continuous experience, has left an indelible impression on them. This is true of children's experiences, which appear in retrospect to be the major markers within the continuum. They can be 'peak experiences' in Maslow's (1954) sense, but they can also be tragedies or surprises or critical incidents that intervene to make up the drama of existence. To refer to them in this way is to underline the essentially dramatic quality of much of children's experience, the emotional toning and ritual context that surrounds a fight or a visit to the dentist or to a relative's house, or a Saturday afternoon at a home fixture. It may also characterise the first encounter with a new 'developmental task' (Havighurst, 1953), which emphasises a particular kind of relationship between experience and development.

A fifth feature which follows from the fourth is that experience as a whole is unpredictable. In this respect it presents its starkest contrast to development. For while development is necessarily basically programmed and only modified by external influences, experience is largely fortuitous and only modified by the effects of past experience. This is particularly important, as will be seen later, in relation to education, since any planning for education must assume some predictability; yet experience is the permanent joker in the pack, varying in both intensity and nature, setting limits to what can be planned.

A sixth characteristic of experience is its inherent proneness to *conflict*. Exposure to one set of experiences can give rise to one set of outcomes; within the totality of experience other individual occurrences may lead to quite a different result. For example, a child may learn in his family that he is subordinate and rather incapable, but in his peer group that he is respected and skilled in ways that the group values. Thus, experience may present problems without suggesting solutions. Moreover, when considered in relation to the fifth feature, the nature of the conflicts is itself always changing, leading to further destabilisation. The devising of solutions then requires learning that goes beyond experience.

This last point indicates a final feature, namely that experience is no more capable than development of acting as a substitute for education. The old Latin tag *experientia docet* is mischievously ambiguous. It is true that experience does 'teach' particular 'lessons', or rather that particular experiences teach them, but not that it 'educates' in any general or ultimate sense. As with development, so with experience, there has to be a counterpoint with curriculum.

## Some Experiential Approaches to Primary Education

In view of the prominence given to experience in philosophy, at least in the West, it is not surprising that experience, like development, has figured as a central feature of important past theories of education that continue to be influential in the present. It has occupied some place in developmental theories also, because development has to accord some role to experience. But the term 'experiential theory' will here be applied only to those theories which give pride of place to experience.

It is tempting to look for the first instances of experiential theory in the age when empiricism in philosophy was first beginning to develop its modern characteristics, that is, in the seventeenth and eighteenth centuries. In writers of that period it appeared in a partial and tentative shape, closely linked with developmental and idealist notions. Locke, whose philosophical treatises are sometimes regarded as the first clear statement of modern empirical principles, carried over these principles into what he had to say about education[2] more clearly and consistently than has sometimes been appreciated. However, it was not until the emergence of the brash materialism of some eighteenth century writers such as d'Holbach, Helvétius and Hartley that experience was given a central role. Influenced by a sensationist psychology which seemed to offer infinite possibilities to the educator, they outlined a pedagogy that would transcend, at least for some people, the limitations of development. They implied that if children were given a carefully selected set of experiences, they would be conditioned into good citizenship and the good life. They did not, of course, specify how the educator himself would be conditioned, or how he would be able to decide what citizenship or what life would be good. All of these writers were working within the optimistic climate of the Enlightenment, and although they did not concern themselves specifically with primary education, their prescriptions for the primary stage were part and parcel of their general approach.

The emergence of Kant's 'critical philosophy' in the latter part of the century altered the philosophical climate itself. It now became more usual to regard the mind as having some powers beyond the limitations of space and time, thus offering a new clarification of the age-old question, 'How can human beings feel that they are free to think and to act, if in fact their thoughts and actions are determined?' To Kant, these powers of thought and action lay outside the realm of rigid cause and effect. That being so, it was possible for Kant and his successors to posit a new and more powerful role for the teacher, whose own thoughts and actions were regarded as outside the pressures of the material world.

One of the most impressive experiential theories was developed at this time by J.F. Herbart. Despite some logical weaknesses it provided a model that could explain and defend the role of the teacher as instructor. In its simplest terms it assumed that the mind was not a physical organ, like the brain, but that in each individual it was initially very simple, little more than a capacity to exist and react. Thus the developmental element was minimised. Herbart here took a stance that was consciously different from the approach of Rousseau and Pestalozzi. Instead, he indicated how a planned pedagogy selected from experience and from what his translators call 'intercourse' could literally build up the mind in such a way that it would acquire desirable knowledge, and thereby also desirable morality. His was a complex theory that defies summary, but this is the part of it that is most closely related to experience[3].

During the nineteenth century Herbart's ideas were temporarily superseded by other experiential theories, particularly those associated with the utilitarian philosophers such as Bentham and Mill. In a sense they continued the optimistic sensationist approach of the Enlightenment, with its belief in economic and social salvation by means of controlled experience. In their case the importance of primary education was clearly brought out because of their association with the beginnings of universal elementary education in England and elsewhere. It provided some justification for the jejune kinds of experience on which universal elementary education depended: later, Herbart's theories were also adapted (and debased) for the same purpose. What Herbart himself had to say about primary education was limited, but related to his own experience. In particular he emphasised the importance of exposure to the great themes of classical and European culture as a civilising experience for younger children.

The emergence in the United States, later in the nineteenth century, of a new kind of philosophy resulted in a new and much more comprehensive theory of experience in education, one which has been particularly influential during the past decades. The principal contributor to this theory was John Dewey. Building on the thought of others in the experiential and also in the developmental tradition, he evolved what he regarded as an essentially dynamic view of education. He accepted that individuals have important developmental properties, but laid much more emphasis on the value of experience. The particular originality of his view was the way in which he envisaged the role of experience. Unlike Herbart, he did not think of it as something judiciously and expertly contrived by others. Rather, he regarded experience as something to be created communally by children in a protected environment, something which would develop outwards in ever widening circles until it led into the intellectual achievements and social organisation appropriate to an evolving democracy. This he did not regard as an automatic process. In his own words: 'The central problem of an education based on experience is to select the kind of present experiences that live fruitfully and creatively in subsequent experience' (1938, pp. 27-8). Thus, the role of the teacher is not to build the learner, but to clear the path for the learners, together, to build themselves and each other. By observing the group and by enacting the principles of 'continuity' and 'interaction' which he regarded as essential to any theory of experience, teachers would improve the quality of experience itself. The central importance attached by Dewey to this process is embodied in his definition of education itself as the continuing reconstruction of experience (1916).

During and since his lifetime Dewey's experiential theory has become linked with what is generally known as progressive education and with the emphasis on learning by doing and through discovery. For this reason, perhaps, the central significance of experience in his writing has sometimes been obscured. Or maybe it is because a rather superficial espousal of 'activity', under the progressive label, has been easier to undertake than the thoroughgoing rigour of the experiential approach, especially at the primary stage.

At the same time, criticisms of this approach have not been lacking. According to the experiential view, a skilful selection of stimuli should lead to a smooth expansion of cognitive and social perspectives. In practice this is not necessarily the case: the conflict component in experience may instead become dominant. Again, the mere selection of experiences within those accessible to children may be insufficient without the introduction of others, which constitutes a concession to Herbart's point of view. There are many socially useful ideas which children will not encounter without direct intervention or even direct instruction. Other writers, equally aware of the importance of experience especially in personal/social development, have preferred to follow Durkheim[4] in prescribing much more closely what a teacher should do, while also building up the status of the teacher at the primary level to something approaching that of a lay priest.

It is appropriate here to refer also to an influential contemporary contribution to educational theory which can be classified as experiential, namely Bruner's 'theory of instruction'[5]. In a sense this is a lineal successor to Herbart's theory, which also emphasised instruction rather than development. It is, however, a much more sophisticated theory, well grounded in modern psychological knowledge derived from empirical research. In evolving it Bruner was well aware of Dewey's ideas and also of the importance of accommodating to developmental characteristics. As was indicated in Chapter 1, he evolved his own set of stages, namely a sequence from 'iconic' through 'enactive' to 'symbolic' representation. Yet this sequence was subordinated in practice to the presentation of a balanced series of experiences seen at its clearest and most impressive in the social studies curriculum designed for the older primary stage under the title *Man, a Course of Study*. Bruner maintained that this course, presenting a selective recapitulation of some aspects of evolution, would enable children to experience their own humanity more adequately and would thus lead them to live their lives more fully. As he put it: 'I think a theory of development must be linked both to a theory of knowledge and to a theory of instruction, or be doomed to triviality' (1966, p. 31).

It may be a moot point whether Bruner's is a theory of experience in the same sense as Dewey's. I rather think it is; but it is one that brings out the need to emphasise the interaction between experience and development in a different way because of Bruner's emphasis on the centrality of instruction.

All the writers considered here have tended to overlook one rather obvious consideration, namely that of the duration and *range* of experience that children have. It starts before they go to school, continues alongside schooling when they do go, and is maintained afterwards. Even within school it exists lustily alongside whatever intervention the school itself undertakes in the social experience of children. More recent studies, such as those by Woods and Hammersley (1977), give ethnographic pictures of children's experience in schools, but still largely ignore the autonomous experience encountered in corridors and playgrounds, at bus stops and behind hedges. Significantly, it is sociologists and anthropologists, together with a few psychologists, who have thrown most light on this essential aspect of experience, its dominance in the lives of children, and the rules and procedures by which they regulate their own and each other's lives as they move slowly up through the age-levels. Yet this is the very stuff of experience, and any actual school programme can only contrive experiences that are meaningful if that wider experience is taken into account. In the course of planning the experiences that a school can contrive, it is easy to overlook those that are already present in children's lives.

It is therefore also easy to overlook some of those characteristics of experience that were mentioned earlier. If it is unpredictable, then the most assiduous follower of Herbart or of Dewey will not be able to go more than a certain distance towards planning what experience an individual is to have. Neither of them really allows for an attack of measles, or the death of a pet, or the movement or termination of a father's job by a firm. Neither of them really allows for crazes or bullying or family holidays. Yet all of these are parts of experience. Again, if it is prone to generate serial conflict, then resolutions of that conflict require other approaches which may be easy to describe verbally, but are not easy to implement in practice.

Experience can thus be viewed both as a major basis of education, and as something outside education. In fact, one of these kinds of experience, the one found in formal education, is a subset of the other. It is a very special, planned, purposive subset, but a subset none the less. If it becomes necessary to refer specifically to the wider kind, that will be termed 'general experience'.

It is now appropriate to look for a term to designate the subset. It cannot be called 'educational experience', since much experience that is educational occurs outside formal education altogether. It cannot be called 'school experience' either, since some experience in school is not 'educational' in this sense. The only term that approaches adequacy is 'curricular experience', and this is appropriate only if curriculum is widely defined. The next chapter will be concerned with curriculum and hence with curricular experience. At this stage the important point to emphasise is the relationship between curricular experience and general experience. It could be epitomised by an irreverent adaptation of the dictum of Dewey's already quoted, thus: 'The central problem of an education based on experience is to select the kind of present *curricular* experiences that live fruitfully and creatively in subsequent *curricular and general* experiences.' Since Dewey was concerned to explain what he meant by the role of experience in education, I hope that he would excuse this exegesis of his text.

Whatever theory of experience is adopted, the importance of experience in general as a basic contributor to the process of education is evident. Moreover, in all of these approaches it is clear that experience is not something external to be passively endured, but something that becomes part of the person. The subjective aspect of experience, whether viewed in the Herbartian or in the Deweian tradition, becomes eventually a part of the self, and a much more idiosyncratic feature than the genetically programmed uniqueness of development. It constructs the world within which each child's schooling takes place, and each child's schooling has to come to terms with it.

## Notes

1. See, for example, the arguments developed by Curtis and Mays (1978).
2. His principal contribution to educational thought was *Some Thoughts Concerning Education*, first published in 1693, (Garforth, 1964). This was followed in the last years of his life with an essay *On the Conduct of the Understanding* (Garforth, 1966), which was deliberately related in title to his major philosophical treatise *Essays on the Human Understanding* (1690). See also Adamson (1922).
3. Herbart's contribution has in recent years been rather under-estimated. One of the best summaries of his theory is to be found in the chapter on Herbart in R.R. Rusk, *Doctrines of the Great Educators*, revised by J. Scotland (Macmillan, 1979). Herbart's own major work was his *Allgemeine Pädagogik* (1806), translated by H.M. and E. Felkin as *The Science of Education* (Swann Sonnenschein, 1904).
4. Emile Durkheim has not usually received his due as a contributor to *educational* theory. The most finely wrought expression of his conception of primary education is

in *L'Éducation Morale*, which he developed during the first decade of the twentieth century and which is available as *Moral Education*, tr. E.K. Wilson and H. Schnurer (New York, Free Press, 1961).

5. This aspect of Bruner's theory is most clearly expressed in *Towards a Theory of Instruction* (Cambridge, Mass., Belknap Press, 1966).

# 3 CURRICULUM

Development and experience are topics familiar to philosophers and to all who ponder on human affairs. Curriculum is a different kind of phenomenon. Any observer of children, or of human beings in general, can come to conclusions about development and experience without going near an establishment of formal education. For development and experience can both take place without involving education, though they cannot be a substitute for education. Curriculum, on the other hand, belongs exclusively to education. Whatever else needs discussing about curriculum, it is not necessary to ask whether or not it is part of education. It is. What is more, the work of Ashton *et al* (1975) indicates that it is a part on which teachers have distinctive and divergent views.

Controversy about curriculum begins at the point at which the question is put, 'What part of education?' Traditionally, the school curriculum has been regarded as a course (the word itself originally meant the course for a chariot race) and also as an aggregate, or in Bernstein's phrase, a 'collection'[1] of subjects. These school subjects have borne a recognisable, though not a one-to-one, relationship with the disciplines of higher study and research. Thus, there is a discipline called mathematics, and a school subject called mathematics which figures in both primary and secondary education. If somebody makes a major innovation in the discipline called mathematics, then eventually that innovation makes some impact on mathematics in schools. However, as soon as other disciplines are considered, the relationship between these and school subjects becomes a little more uneasy. 'English' means something quite different at different levels. 'Science' is an entity at the primary stage, a subject group at the secondary level, and a bewildering range of specialisms where academic disciplines are concerned. Other languages make their entry usually at the secondary level, not usually simultaneously, and with quite a different emphasis from what is customary in higher education. As for art and craft, music and religious education, the relationship is still more distant, while an entire range of legal, technological and medical studies have no school counterpart at all. Nevertheless, the description of curriculum as an aggregate of subjects is a meaningful one, and indeed one that until quite recently was the only one current.

Now, however, it is possible to think of curriculum as a much wider process. It is interesting that a whole range of what were once called 'extra-curricular activities' such as games and chess and drama and camping are now regarded as part of this wider curriculum. Beyond this again there is the area of informal social control and value-transmission now usually known as the hidden curriculum. In this wider view curriculum becomes all the planned and intended programme of a school, including what is not consciously designed but forms part of the school's ethos and unwritten assumptions. Within this wider definition subjects themselves may be viewed in a different way, or merged into groups or into a totality. Thus, what once seemed a simple feature of education has become a much more complex and subtle matter. Instead of being just a function of general theories of education, curriculum has itself become the subject of theoretical interpretation.

There are nowadays many excellent introductions to curriculum theory and its various branches[2]. As with development and experience, it would be pretentious to try to do more in a single chapter than to single out elements of curriculum theory that are most relevant to the primary curriculum, and to indicate their range and variety.

First, there are theories based on the nature of knowledge or, more adequately, understanding. One such theory is lucidly and cogently expressed in the writings of Hirst[3]. The essential point in such theories is that there are forms or styles of understanding which are independent of individual knowers and which are also each conceptually independent of the others, with truth-criteria of its own. Thus, for example, empirical or scientific understanding is something that constitutes one part of everybody's experience but is also distinct from other forms. A list of such forms of understanding would normally include, alongside empirical or scientific understanding, modes that are mathematical, logical, literary, historical, aesthetic, moral and religious, with a distinct social-scientific mode possibly constituting yet another. It is a list such as this, with its necessary liability to slight modifications in detail, that will be implied in the subsequent discussion. The forms will however be deliberately styled as *forms of understanding and endeavour* rather than of knowledge, since they represent broad categories of mental activity and not mere cognition.

A curriculum based on this kind of assumption must necessarily have a timeless character, since the 'forms' themselves are considered to reflect, in large measure, the structure of mind. Therefore, it must show what Eggleston (1977) terms a 'received perspective'. It must also include, for everybody, some introduction or 'initiation' into all of the forms of understanding and endeavour that figure in whatever list is preferred, at any particular moment, by a particular writer. The slight variability that is implied by this subjectivity of definition is not a serious flaw in the argument for a curriculum based on *forms*, for the measure of agreement between writers is high, and indeed could be raised higher through the outcome of a sustained programme of research using techniques such as factor analysis or cluster analysis to distinguish between the basic components. Some limited studies on these lines have already been undertaken. It could, of course, emerge that the forms themselves appear to change over time, as cultural conditions alter; but the forms approach in its stronger embodiment would not permit of such change; and in any case any change that did become evident would be very slight from year to year, or even from century to century.

The relevance of forms of understanding has become established in official policy, notably in the documents issued by Her Majesty's Inspectorate in England and Wales on the secondary curriculum (DES, 1977). At the primary stage, however, the forms-of-understanding approach appears to falter somewhat. It seems more realistic to speak of historical or scientific understanding at the age of 16 than at the age of 6. Even in physical and aesthetic activities the separate consideration of forms of endeavour may seem a trifle pretentious for infants. Yet Ashton's (1975) survey of aims in primary education made use of this kind of categorising, while Dearden (1968) has enunciated a classic case for basing consideration of the primary curriculum on forms of understanding. For if the forms really are logically distinct and independent of individual interests, then they must also be independent of development. In one sense they must also be independent of experience, since they imply an *a priori* assumption that experience will lead toward a commonly agreed view of knowledge and experience as it 'is'. Their claim to determine curriculum, even for the youngest, depends on the belief that human knowledge is, and must be, like that.

Another feature of the usual lists of forms of understanding is that they bear quite a close relationship to subjects. Language, history, science, mathematics, physical education, moral education, religious education, art and craft—all seem very close to one or other of the forms, although others, 'fields' such as geography and (in some formulations) some of the social sciences, straddle them. It is, however, important to remember that the forms are much more than a refurbished description of subjects. For the assumption is not that subjects suggested forms, but rather that forms have gradually, in the course of human history, given rise to subjects and to disciplines, and to the whole articulated structure of the traditional curriculum and its modifications. There could be slow modifications in subjects, as in the forms themselves, in the course of long historical periods, and rather different versions in different cultures, but within the dominant modern Western culture, they are regarded as valid, and that is sufficient for most practical purposes: so the argument goes.

Granted these features of the forms approach to curriculum, it is not surprising that primary education is one of the areas in which it has been challenged. One of the ways in which a challenge can be mounted is to envisage curriculum as something wholly derived from the nature of the learner rather than from the forms of understanding or endeavour. In Chapter 1 the inadequacy of this possibility has been considered. It may be development, but it is not education, and therefore it cannot really be curriculum. However, as was indicated in the discussion of experience in Chapter 2, there is a more promising approach which regards understanding as constructed anew by every learner, with the accumulated intellectual achievements of mankind as a principal part of the available cognitive resources rather than as an imperative that must be obeyed when curriculum is developed. This will be termed, as is now the custom, a *process* approach, and has something in common with Eggleston's 'restructuring perspective' (1977). On this analysis anyone who chooses to disregard these achievements may be an idiot, but he is not a transgressor. Each individual constructs his intellectual world in basically the same way as the creative artist or scientist or thinker who is at the margin of intellectual advance. The formulation of hypotheses and experiments, the active means of discovery of verification, are characteristic of the early primary years in their own way, just as they are characteristic of the community of scholars and scientists. Re-discovery proceeds by the same means as discovery. So, as Blenkin and Kelly (1981) indicate with particular lucidity, though Dewey would have agreed, the proper approach to the primary curriculum in a scientific culture should be through learning by discovery, not through an exploration of pre-specified forms. Moreover, the curriculum itself should be shaped according to research, not only on its components as was once the case, (Fleming, 1946) but on its very basis (Kelly, 1981).

There is nothing startlingly new in this claim. It has been characteristic of the progressive tradition in education, especially primary education, during the past half-century, and it informs much of the Plowden Report (CACE, 1967), which is widely regarded as representing that tradition, though the report itself is much less bold and consistent than its critics sometimes assert. It can be readily accommodated to both development and experience, for it allows the individual's discovery of knowledge to be proportioned to his development and responsive to his experience. It can comprehend an integrated day in the infant school and a pattern of partial differentiation into broad subject-areas at the upper primary or middle-years level. Even at the primary stage, however, it may imply some of the practical difficulties identified with the integrated curriculum by Bernstein (1975), including in particular the professional demands it makes upon teachers. But the principal point remains that it cannot meet the objections of those who, having considered all aspects of the question, still feel that the specific claims of forms of understanding and endeavour are too powerful to be set aside.

There is also a third approach to curriculum that receives widespread support. It may be called the *social-imperatives* approach. Unlike the first two, it is concerned less with individual knowledge and endeavour and more with the needs of society. The relationship between individual and social aims is one of the perennial issues in education, and this approach is one of its recent manifestations. The emergence of the modern secular state has been accompanied, almost inevitably, by schemes for the education of suitable citizens. A sequence can be traced from pre-revolutionary and revolutionary France and the newly independent USA, through the builders of national systems in nineteenth-century Europe, to twentieth-century regimes of the Right and Left in Europe and beyond. Much of the writing on this theme has been of a trivial, polemic or merely administrative nature, but there have been examples of coherent philosophical thought about education and social needs which have risen above the level of most of this literature. They include Durkheim's vision of secular moral education, Kerschensteiner's programme for technical understanding, and designs for different kinds of political education by writers as different as Gentile and

Gramsci[4]. Not all of these have spelled out the content of the curriculum in detail; not all of them have indicated what pedagogy would be appropriate. Some have done both, and all have implications for both.

In contemporary writings there are two main threads in the social-imperatives approach. The first is concerned primarily with technical competence and know-how. It lies behind many of the calls for more science and technology in the curriculum. Though, of course, science also figures prominently in the forms and process approaches, technology lags behind in both, and it is its direct instrumental value that brings it into prominence in this third approach. Indeed, some of the call for emphasis on an agreed core curriculum in English education, which would bring it closer to other systems, is derived from this kind of instrumental competence. The other thread is frankly political and ideological, and is seen at its most conspicuous in a Marxist state where compulsory and exclusive political education is invariably introduced, and almost as visibly in a fundamentalist Islamic state, though it exists widely in other societies too, even in those which officially deny it. The relationship between these two kinds of social-imperatives curriculum is significant. Few societies with overt political curricula omit technological elements; indeed, in Marxist-Leninist education there is often a polytechnical element introduced for social and political reasons. Meanwhile, in Western societies a technological emphasis may be accompanied by official displeasure towards overt political education. All of these considerations apply to primary as well as secondary education, though in the process they may result in a relative depreciation of the importance of primary education as such.

A further modification of this social-imperatives approach to curriculum should also be mentioned, particularly in view of the recent impact that this modification has made. In this modification the construction of knowledge is itself seen, particularly by Marxists and phenomenologists, as essentially the work of social groups. More than that, the intellectual products of scientists and scholars are regarded as the result of social processes rather than as objective achievements. If the primary curriculum is viewed from this angle, it is not enough to conceive it 'in terms of activity and experience', as the 1931 Primary School Report put it (Consultative Committee of the Board of Education, or even to opt for one form of social imperative, because this would only result in, for example, a bourgeois curriculum in the middle-class school, a proletarian curriculum in a working-class school, and a curricular conflict where the cultures are mixed. Other social divisions, for example between town and country, might result in other constructions of understanding and endeavour. Important though it is to recognise the strength of social influence in the building of knowledge, and the difficulty of defining a single social imperative, it is hard to see how this approach can contribute substantially to the making of curricula, for either it implies accepting social differentiation of the curriculum as inevitable, or it involves reinforcing the claims of one social imperative as against others. This might mean imposing middle-class values, as existing formal education is alleged to do, or it might mean substituting working-class values and imposing those, as some might like to do; or it might mean winnowing the culture of any community to define and build on the best of its own values, as Midwinter (1975) once recommended. It is by no means certain that any of these policies would prove either practicable or defensible.

There are, of course, other ways of classifying approaches to curriculum. Richards (1982, Part 1), for example, writing in particular of the primary curriculum, selects four 'ideologies', liberal romanticism, educational conservatism, liberal pragmatism and social democracy, as informing recent thinking about the primary curriculum. The first two of these have something in common with the process and forms-of-understanding approaches respectively, though in the case of educational conservatism much more emphasis is laid on cultural heritage. Liberal pragmatism implies some blend between the two. Social democracy embodies one, but only one, form of social imperative. Kohlberg and Mayer (1972) divide approaches to curriculum into three: progressive, culture-transmission and romantic. This departs rather further from what is suggested here, for the first two both embody something of the process approach, while forms of understanding are rather precariously combined with culture transmission (as in Richards's educational conservatism), and social imperatives are left rather adrift. It would, of course, be possible to cite many other instances of curricular classification, but these two seem especially pertinent to the present discussion. The decision to use the classification based on process, forms of understanding and social imperatives is made because they seem particularly appropriate to a discussion of curriculum in relation to development and experience. Each of these three approaches displays particular characteristics in practice, and these will be considered next.

First, and most important, we should consider what may be described as the dynamics of the curriculum. Here the approach through forms of understanding and endeavour requires a planned introduction to the different forms, allowing all children to sample them, whether for the sake of balanced development or in order to allow a free choice, and free rejection, among them. It is a moot point how far this sampling approach can be planned. It is also problematic whether any particular knowledge-base has prior claim for inclusion among the samples of the forms, or whether this can be left to personal preference or even to chance. Different views could be expressed according to the precise point of view of the individual planner or teacher.

In the second, the process approach, there is no such variability. Here, the emphasis is firmly placed on the activity of the learner. Whatever a child actually learns matters, in this view, less than the process of learning to learn. How a child actually behaves is also, in this view, less important than the process of learning to behave. Put starkly in this way, the strengths and limitations of the process view of curriculum become evident. The process of learning to learn involves emphasis on skills rather than content. The process of learning to behave also involves emphasis on skills rather than patterns. A thorough-going adherent of the process approach really has to defend both. In most cases there is more reluctance to apply a process approach to social norms and behaviour than to intellectual competence.

As for the social-imperatives approach, its dynamic is guided by the product rather than by the process. What a child learns, and how he behaves, is central to the approach, and so the organisation of the curriculum must be such as to minimise and as far as possible neutralise the effects of development and experience alike. This may not imply *Gleichschaltung*, or enforced similarity. It may mean no more than that the official curriculum has to ensure a common basis while allowing development and experience to foster individuality in all other matters. If so, it implies a rather limited, prescriptive and instrumental curriculum, one in which the claims of sequence are not very strong and in which the building blocks can be assembled in a number of alternative ways. The momentum in such a curriculum can be sustained by ritual means, such as an emphasis on year-grading and the prestige associated with promotion, or the privileges attached to particular attainments which may, for instance, facilitate entry to the Young Pioneers. Yet such momentum is extrinsic to the curriculum in a way that is not true of the forms approach, and cannot be true of the process approach.

The next issue concerns the degree of pre-specification that a curriculum requires. Traditionally, a school looked efficient if there was a copper-plate timetable in the Head's desk, indicating what would be done with a class's time during each day, and a syllabus indicating what would be done in each subject during each year. In a forms approach this would be rather more difficult to implement. In a process approach it would be virtually impossible and indefensible, for it would imply foreknowledge of how individuals and groups would discover their reality. In a social-imperatives approach, however, it might well be reinstated, though for rather different reasons.

Similar considerations apply to another form of curriculum planning that has been prominent in recent years, namely planning by objectives. Under the influence of Tyler (1949), Bloom, Krathwohl *et al.* (1956; 1964) and others it has been considered valuable to specify objectives at various levels from particular pieces of teaching up to the formulation of whole courses. Objectives are more focused and attainable than aims, and more flexible than subjects. They have been widely used, especially in secondary and tertiary education, and as will be seen in Chapters 5 and 6, they have figured in some aspects of curriculum planning in primary education too. For the social-imperatives approach, the specification of objectives has wide appeal and applicability. The parallel with management techniques reinforces this appeal. There is also a substantial attraction in objectives for the forms approach.

Even if forms of understanding and endeavour are the basis of the curriculum, pre-specification of objectives may be an inappropriate way of proceeding. For whereas the attainment of a particular concept in mathematics may be aided in this way, a fruitful response to an aesthetic experience may actually be impeded, since the essence of an individual's response may just be that it is not susceptible to planning or prediction. As Stenhouse has said, with reference to secondary education, it may for some purposes be more important to plan inputs than outputs, to provide stimuli than to anticipate responses. In a process approach, however, the formulation of objectives for any purpose can only be very short term. What is more, they can only be spelled out jointly by children and teachers as a part of the curricular process itself, not imposed upon it as a major direction or constraint.

The next aspect of curriculum to be considered is that of skill and concept formation and attainment. Each of our principal approaches to curriculum allows a central place to the cultivation of skills and concepts. To the first two approaches, they are essential for the construction of knowledge and endeavour; to the social-imperatives approach, they are a necessary basis for military, economic and political competence. In practice it is likely that much the same tools and concepts will figure for all these purposes, in particular the skills of language and number and motor control. So it is also not surprising that curriculum theory has given particular attention to the economical formation and attainment of skills and concepts. Sometimes this has taken the form of selecting key skills and concepts regarded as particularly important for the development of others (Taba, 1962). Sometimes this type of approach has been further articulated into a major sequence such as the spiral curriculum advocated by Bruner (1966), justified on psychological grounds. Skill and concept formation is thus central to all the main approaches to curriculum, though justified in each on slightly different grounds.

Much the same is true of the next aspect, that of the social organisation of learning. Although it is more likely that a forms approach and a social-imperatives approach will both be associated with a didactic, teacher-centred organisation while the process approach engenders group work and individual studies, this need not be so. As Dearden (1968) points out, a mixture of methods is appropriate to each approach. A prescribed movement in dance or in a ball-game skill or a rudimentary technological process may be practised by individuals or pairs; a whole class may agree to have their teacher carry out an experiment or to present a videotape on the topic that they are exploring. In each of these cases, too, it is essential that each individual child shall participate meaningfully; it is impossible to justify the education of groups or of societies unless individuals are educated in the process. Yet there are ways in which the three approaches to curriculum do validly diverge in social organisation.

The most marked divergence is between the exercise and the project. The forms approach requires an initiation by some form of participation: the introduction to a musical instrument is perhaps the most usually cited prototype. I suppose it is possible to derive some advantage from merely scraping a violin or plucking a guitar, but unless the instrument is approached in what has come to be the tried and accepted manner, its potential is virtually squandered. That manner in turn involves exercises to stimulate dexterity as well as musical understanding. Similarly, in the social-imperatives approach skill acquisition, or for that matter rudiments of religious observance or of Marxist-Leninist praxis, may well involve the learning of some particular skills. On the other hand the process approach, with its problem-centred characteristics, is typically associated with the project or topic. This has no prescribed form, but can arise from the particular curiosities and powers of individuals or groups. To be sure, it does not always live up to its problem-centred origin. There is quite a difference between 'How do worms live and move?' and 'Our book about roads', because the first of these does at least have the appearance of answering a question, while the latter may be little more than a collection of rather arbitrary transcriptions and cuttings. But if the topic or project is true to its purpose, it is quite a different sort of activity from an exercise[5].

There is also a difference, though not so marked a difference, in the social roles of individuals in the different kinds of activity. In an exercise basically everybody is doing the same. One boy, or girl, may be chosen to show his or her skill in a somersault for the benefit of the class, but that is in order to encourage the rest of the class to learn how to perform a somersault. But in a project there may be genuine division of labour; and this is introduced not so much in order to hasten the completion of the project, as to encourage the learning of social roles in general, as part of learning how to behave in general. The advantage of this element in the process approach is that it enriches the whole business of primary education. The possible disadvantage, which has to be avoided through the teacher's skill, is that some children will be assigned, all too readily, the subordinate roles, and that these roles will be generalised over time into low status within the class.

This last point serves to bring out one remaining contrast between the three types of curriculum, namely the part played in each by the teacher. In the first, the forms approach, the teacher requires two qualities: specific expertise in each form—an ambitious enough claim, in fact—and the ability to introduce children to it. At the secondary stage this can be met by a division of labour at the teacher's own level: often in fact there are several teachers to each form of understanding, even though forms and subjects are not to be exactly equated[6]. The rationale of this division is that the farther children are taken into any form, the greater the demands on the teacher's own skills and knowledge. The implication for the primary teacher, however, is daunting. For it is assumed that below the secondary level most teachers must be capable of introducing most pupils to most of the forms of understanding and endeavour, and that some teachers must be capable of introducing all of their pupils to all of the forms. Not only must they be to some extent versed in all of these forms, they must also have, at least to some extent, the range of skills required to introduce children to all of them. In one sense, indeed, the demand is greater even than this. For there are grounds for thinking that it is the first invitation, the very first step in initiation to a form of understanding or endeavour, that is decisive in influencing subsequent responses.

For the teacher working within the process framework, however, the task is at least equally daunting. Instead of a stock of fairly elementary knowledge and skills, this teacher has to know how to stimulate and organise the thinking and doing of a whole class in such a way as to lead to the collective formulation of a problem, one that has potential for leading on to other and more stimulating problems in its turn, one that 'matches' effectively the powers of the individual or group as a whole, yet allows for individuals to play suitable parts. Then, having made that selection, he or she has to know how to provide, or at least suggest, means for the solution of the problem, and satisfactory ways in which the parts played by all the individuals concerned can be worked out so that their own knowledge and understanding is thereby extended. The intellectual ramifications of the problem have to be recognised, yet confined within the children's powers: there must be no thinking at the level of 'fitting in some geography', or even at the level of satisfying the teacher's own curiosity or bent. In other words, this teacher has to be both a curricular analyst and a social analyst, an expert both in curriculum and in children.

For the teachers working in a social-imperatives curriculum, the role may be a more limited one. However technically demanding their task may be, the major direction of the curriculum is undertaken by others, and much of the specific information they need may be offered to them, or even thrust upon them. To hard-pressed teachers, this may be a deceptively reassuring prospect. Nevertheless, they too must prove themselves competent to handle it according to the guidelines they receive, and this may be no mean task. What is more, failure may be correspondingly more conspicuous, and the penalties for failure correspondingly greater.

Thus, all three approaches make demands on primary teachers that are, on any showing, sufficient to dispel the notion that their task is a humble or a humdrum affair that can be easily learned or half-heartedly implemented. What is more, the teacher of the calibre required for any of these models of curriculum must also be capable of understanding, and coming to a decision about, problems of curriculum. To operate effectively in each model requires the kind of understanding characteristic of a profession, a point that will be developed further in Chapter 9.

In these first three chapters the three elements of development, experience and curriculum have been separately considered. Though their interrelations have been indicated here and there, for the most part they have merely been, as it were, juxtaposed on the table of educational discourse. But it is of the essence of educational discourse that decisions have to be taken in the light of that discourse. Three separate essays on separate topics do not take us very far. The following chapter embodies one attempt to bring the three elements together in a coherent manner and to formulate an approach to development, experience and curriculum in primary education that could be of assistance to teachers who have to decide what to do, and why they should do it, in particular situations.

Before that approach is outlined, it must be remembered that this is only one way in which the three elements can be brought together. Many other ways are possible, and the way exemplified here is based on values which necessarily tolerate others unlike themselves. Other people would choose other ways, with different justifications. In a field such as primary education there is bound to be diversity of views; in a value-system such as this, diversity is bound to be permitted. What matters is that in each case those views should be thoroughly thought out, and justified on grounds which exemplify both intellectual awareness and personal integrity. Children deserve nothing less.

## Notes

1. Basil Bernstein, one of the most fertile of contemporary thinkers on the social significance of education, has at different times emphasised different aspects of his own thinking. His analysis of curriculum is clearly expressed in *Class, Codes and Control—3—Towards a Theory of Educational Transmissions* (1975).

2. Two of the most comprehensive general studies are those by Stenhouse (1975)

and Kelly (1982). A useful introduction is the handbook by A. and H. Nicholls (1972). Denis Lawton and Malcolm Skilbeck touch on many of the main curricular issues in their numerous books.

3. Notably in *Knowledge and the Curriculum* (Routledge & Kegan Paul, 1975).

4. Durkheim's writing is referred to in Chapter 2, note 4. Georg Kerschensteiner's work in Munich before and after the First World War earned him widespread respect for his thoughtful emphasis on the educative potential of technical studies. Giovanni Gentile came near to providing a philosophical justification for education along Fascist lines in Italy and elsewhere between the world wars. Antonio Gramsci was one of the most distinguished exponents of a neo-Marxist approach to education in the West, and pointed out the fallacy implicit in working-class rejection of the intellectual content of middle-class curricula (see Entwistle (1979).

5. The project method has been associated with the process approach to curriculum, and also with Dewey's experiential approach. Since Dewey's time, many books have been written about projects and topics, many of them designed to offer positive practical advice. At the time when this book is in preparation, a Schools Council project is under way at the University of Nottingham School of Education, under the direction of Professor J.F. Eggleston and Trevor Kerry, *Developing Pupils' Thinking Through Topic Work* at the primary stage.

6. The conventional meaning of 'form teacher' as used in English secondary schools is obviously not implied here.

# 4 ONE APPROACH TO PRIMARY EDUCATION: AN ENABLING CURRICULUM

For each school, each class, each child, somebody has to decide on one approach to primary education which will be, on some set of criteria, suitable. In some societies the choice is made centrally; in some, within individual schools; or in individual classes, which is not the same thing. At whatever level the choice is to be made, a process of choice is necessary, and in this chapter an attempt is made to indicate how a process of choice can be applied to the three elements of development, experience and curriculum in order to derive one legitimate approach, and to indicate how others might be derived.

To do so implies an avowed choice of a set of values; or rather, it assumes that a set of values has already been chosen. No education is possible without a set of values, and any education which purports to be value-free is likely to be based on hidden values of its own. Similarly, any approach to education which claims to be entirely derived from theories of development, or experience, or of curriculum is unlikely to be adequate. For either it is based on a fallacious argument, such as that because education is related to development, therefore education ought to depend on development; or it is based on an argument derived from other and still more basic premises. The approach indicated in the present chapter is not a finely wrought, philosophically complete exposition. It rests simply on one basic assumption.

This assumption is that democratic attitudes are preferable to other attitudes. More explicitly, this means that decisions negotiated within groups are preferable to decisions imposed by superiors; that individual views should not be submerged by group views; and that no group should impose itself by any kind of force on any other group. Such a set of values is somewhat idealistic as well as being somewhat imprecise; but it does have meaning and is clearly distinguishable from authoritarian attitudes.

This basic assumption is reinforced by two others. One of these is derived from the Judaic-Christian tradition. It implies a way of valuing people which can and indeed must transcend the democratic stance, but is here regarded as fully compatible with it and adding something to it, something which at the least implies a kind of compassionate concern. The remaining assumption is simply that all unbridled ideological positions are in themselves dangerous. At the least, they imply a claim to certainty; at the most, they lead people to claim powers over others that are quite incompatible with the first two assumptions. Moreover, ideological programmes are almost always pretentious and fallacious, and when their feet of clay appear, their adherents are left adrift and bewildered.

It will, of course, be claimed that this position is itself ideological; but that is not so within the meaning given here to ideology. My position is one that is continuously corrigible in its own terms, adjusting to different ideas and new emphases within the democratic framework, and finding new ways of valuing people in a compassionate way.

It may also be claimed that this position is outmoded, even disproved. In 1983 there are political currents on both Right and Left which regard this type of democratic attitude as context-bound, discredited, blind to stark economic, political or social realities. That is why 'liberal' and 'social-democratic' are often used as pejoratives far beyond their ostensible political connotations. For my part I do not regard this standpoint as outmoded or incapable of leading to a somewhat juster social order. Rather, I think it is one of the least unlikely means of attaining a somewhat juster social order. At the same time, as a Christian, I do not believe that any secular stance can in itself hold the key to social perfectibility.

With this in mind, it is possible to look again at development, experience and curriculum, to bring them together into a coherent approach to primary education.

First, the relative roles and importance of development and experience have to be judged. Development, in its three aspects, can be taken as anything from a set of negative limitations, reluctantly acknowledged, to a source of guidance, uncritically accepted. From the point of view enunciated in this chapter, development has to be regarded as something positive. Individual children do each have some inbuilt programme, and each programme is different. This can be deduced from principles of heredity, but also from observation. An attempt to impose a uniform, or even a non-uniform, pattern of education that does not take serious account of developmental considerations violates any concept of democracy as it has been described here.

Experience can be taken as implying anything from the unpredictable partner of development in an interactive process to a *tabula rasa* from which heredity can be, for all practical purposes, expunged. From the point of view enunciated in this chapter, the second of these possibilities has some emotional appeal, but it is contrary to much of the evidence that arises from direct observation as well as from systematic study. The limits of experience have to be recognised, and they are limits set by development. Moreover, undue emphasis on its potential can easily involve brash attempts to re-mould individuals and societies, disregarding both the evidence in favour of developmental factors and the strains and misfortunes resulting for individuals when those factors are disregarded. On the other hand, over-emphasis on the inevitability of some features of development can result in a belittling of the power of experience to effect any real change, so that those who are alleged to benefit from the developmental advantages drawn from their innate endowment may continue to do so. Thus, a democratic approach requires caution in the face of either extreme view of experience.

When primary education is considered in particular, development and experience both claim consideration. Both appear with more clarity than in secondary or tertiary education, where questions of content and organisation so readily tend to supervene. Young children's development is so palpable; their experience so relatively uncomplicated. What is more, the mutual dependence of development and experience is shown with particular clarity. The third element, curriculum, should thus be approached on the further assumption that *there should be a balanced interaction between development and experience.* However, that does not mean that there should be some precise Newtonian calculation of their relative importance. The balance refers not to a once-for-all weighting of their significance, but to a continuing process which gives the predominance now to the one, now to the other, in particular situations, but which is directed in the long run to the best outcome for each individual child. It also implies a re-assertion of the obvious but frequently overlooked truth that the interaction between development and experience begins before curriculum, continues alongside curriculum, and extends beyond curriculum. Moreover, curriculum, though it builds upon experience and constitutes that part of experience that falls within formal education, is still only a part of experience.

The role of curriculum considered in the rest of this book is that it is *planned intervention in the interaction between development and experience.* This is to be taken to mean that curricular experience is planned intervention between development and general experience. For the sake of simplicity, henceforth the nicety of meaning will be overlooked, and 'experience' will denote 'general experience' while 'curriculum' will be used as shorthand for 'curricular experience'. In other words, the relationships spelled out in Chapter 2 will be borne in mind while a simplified terminology is used.

If the terminology is kept simple, the relationships are far from simple. For there is an ongoing interaction between development and curriculum, and between experience and curriculum, as well as between development and experience. The difference between curriculum and the other elements is the obvious one, that development and experience are continuous, whereas curriculum is substantially confined to the place and time of formal education. This does not mean that its importance is proportionately reduced. The pressures of society throw into relief what goes on in school; curriculum as a whole, unlike development or experience as a whole, is designed to make a positive impact on children; and curriculum is fashioned in such a way as to interact positively with development and experience and to maximise their value for children.

As we have already seen, many of the most far-seeing among those who emphasise the importance of development in education stress, as Montessori did, the necessity of curriculum as a means of optimising development. Similarly, many of the ablest and most thoughtful advocates of experience in education stress that curriculum is itself a major component of experience. As Dewey said of education: 'It is that reconstruction or reorganisation of experience which adds to experience, and which increases ability to direct the course of subsequent experience' (1916, p. 76). Thus curriculum is both a part of experience and a means of extending experience.

In fact, curriculum is essential to both development and experience. This is an essential part of the point of view advocated in this chapter. The relationship between the three elements can be epitomised in the model shown in Figure 4.1.

But of course the process is a dynamic sequence, and may perhaps be more appropriately illustrated in the form of a highly formalised flow chart (figure 4.2). In Figure 4.2, $D_{0..1..2}$ stands for steps in development; $E_{0..1..2}$ for episodes in (general) experience; and $C_{1..2}$ for units of curriculum (i.e. curricular experience). The use of the zero subscript in the developmental and experiential series but not in the curricular series is deliberate: it emphasises that

Figure 4.1: Static Relationship between Development, Experience and Curriculum

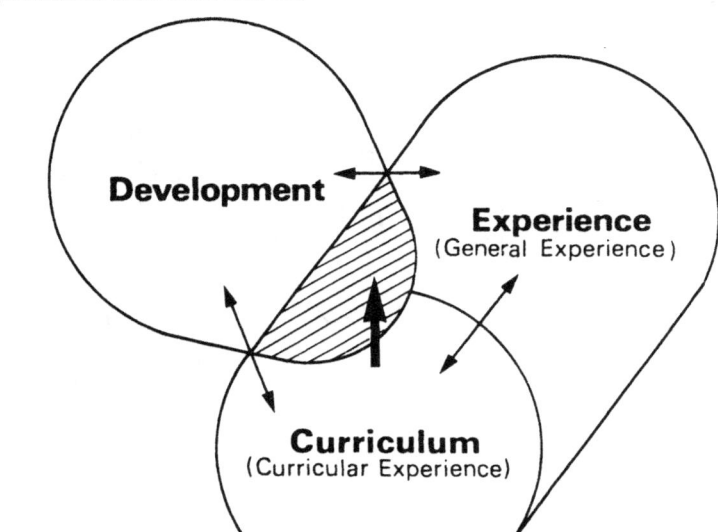

development and experience are active before curriculum begins. Similarly, if the series is continued to the end of formal education, the final curricular unit might be entitled $C_n$ but there would be after that $D_{n+1..n+2}$ and also $E_{n+1..n+2}$ continuing throughout life.

Of course, this whole diagram is immensely simplified. All sorts of development and experience, and many curricular units, are in play simultaneously. I am quite aware of this. But there are times when a concentrated notation can convey the essence of a process.

It is necessary now to turn back to the three main approaches to curriculum discussed in the previous chapter, in order to consider which of them is most promising for the purpose of planned intervention in the interaction between development and experience.

The curricular principle least appropriate for this purpose is the one derived from social imperatives. A democratic approach cannot envisage children as primarily operatives (to use the nineteenth-century term), or as voters, soldiers, parishioners or even as citizens. Yet it is not as simple as this. A democratic education must at least try to ensure the conditions in which it can exist. It may

Figure 4.2: Dynamic Relationship between Development, Experience and Curriculum

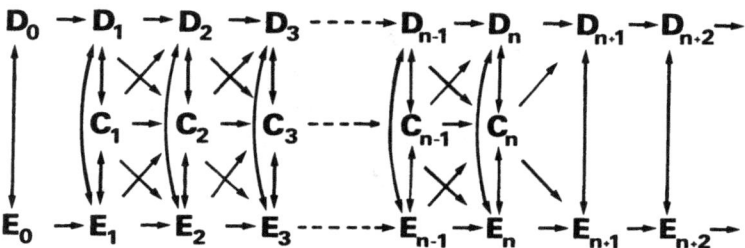

permit the attachment of individuals to certain social, political or religious creeds, each of which would wish to act as the cuckoo in the democratic nest; but it cannot encourage this process or even regard it with indifference. Some positive emphasis on democratic values and their cultivation is a minimum requirement. It is a far cry from the contrived insistence on unquestioning acceptance of any one creed.

There is also another way in which the social-imperatives approach cannot be dismissed too lightly. There is a reciprocal relationship between society and formal education which goes beyond the transmission of ideas. In the accountability formulation that has become familiar in recent times, no society can live beyond its means, or will into being an educational provision or policy without stopping to consider how it can be implemented, financially and administratively. The importance of economic activity can claim inclusion in a curriculum for this reason alone. On the other hand, it is unreasonable to maintain that its inclusion should take the form of prescriptive initiation into particular skills and activities without reference to the general social order within which they are to be conducted, or to some consideration of how that social order could be criticised and ameliorated.

On a smaller scale, local communities can make claims of their own. Indeed, when local communities are in a situation of particular social malaise, for example through depopulation or unemployment, a curriculum that attempts to disregard these circumstances might well be in its turn disregarded. Similarly, there may be specific claims for curricular adjustment in rural areas, or those with particular problems of bilingualism or of a mix of cultures. All of these circumstances represent social imperatives of one kind or another, and all present much the same curricular dilemma. If too little notice is taken of those circumstances, the curriculum may prove irrelevant or even unworkable; if too much notice is taken of them, it may act as a means of reinforcing the separateness of the local community from the wider society and even as an obstacle in the path of those who would like to transcend its barriers and to take part in the wider society.

The social-imperatives approach does, therefore, make considerable demands upon any democratic approach to primary education. However, the positive importance of the forms and process approaches is greater.

The forms approach, in its stronger embodiment, makes claims almost irrespective of development and experience, claims derived from a totally objective view of knowledge and endeavour. But in its more flexible form it looks upon curriculum as consisting of broad areas of understanding and endeavour which have emerged within the historic process in almost all societies, certainly within those which today have established systems of formal education. This more flexible version of the forms approach does not make elaborate claims for the individual forms, nor for their precise definition, but it does assert that they are fundamentally distinct ways of understanding and endeavour, the omission of any one of which would impoverish education. This is a little less forceful than the argument based on initiation or on civic need, but it does imply that personal development and the expansion of experience require some exposure to all of them. Moreover, there is a sense in which they can claim to be themselves a part of the structure of development and experience.

However, the main emphasis has to be laid on the third approach to curriculum, the process approach. This is because if the purpose is to uphold individuals and their autonomous fulfilment, then what matters is how they discover understanding and endeavour for themselves. To combine this with a flexible version of the forms is not a contradiction. The particular acts of co-operative learning and endeavour involved in the various elements in the curriculum can, and should, be based on ways of discovery that are related to development and experience. The choice of curricular areas, or indeed of the possible range of problems and activities within them, cannot be left entirely to an arbitrary process of discovery which, in practice, is often devoid of purposive sequence and structure or of the expertise needed to guide, interpret and stimulate that discovery. In other words, at the level of micro-planning of individual episodes of learning, the process approach makes strong demands; at the level of macro-planning of curriculum, it requires interaction with forms, and to some extent with social imperatives.

There is one further important consideration. In the preceding discussion there was some danger of regarding the curriculum as static, or at any rate of giving priority to the curriculum as it appears at the later primary stage. But primary education has to be considered as a whole, and begins at a chronological age when, on any showing, development and experience preclude the clear differentiation of the curriculum into forms. To begin with, it must be much more of a totality. Differentiation into separate kinds of activity is itself a part of the curriculum process at the primary stage. More than that, it is something that forms part of guided discovery. For this reason the emphasis on the process approach to curriculum at the primary stage is further strengthened. Whatever arguments might be applied in secondary or even in later primary education, the primary curriculum as a whole has to take account of what happens at the very start.

Hitherto, some of the characteristics of a worthwhile primary curriculum have been indicated: its relation to development and experience, its prime but not exclusive dependence on the process model, and its modification according to age. It has already been defined as a balanced intervention in the interaction between development and experience, with the proviso that the interaction takes place between all three elements. What is needed now, before the discussion is taken further, is a more succinct term for the kind of curriculum that is to be elaborated.

The term I suggest is: *the enabling curriculum.*[1]

If we are to speak of an enabling curriculum, then it is necessary to say what it enables, and why it enables more than would be the case if it were not introduced.

The verdict about what this curriculum enables must depend on the approach that has been advocated in this chapter. Thus, first, it has to be a curriculum that enables development and experience to take place beneficially. It must provide additional equipment that arises through development beyond the powers of the human organism as such, development that can arise only through the stimulus of a systematic process of construction of reality strengthened by awareness of widely accepted forms of understanding and endeavour. It must also provide opportunities for the expansion and reflective scrutiny of experience, within a social context that ensures that development and experience are social as well as individual.

Beyond this, it must also enable each individual to become a person with an emerging set of values and ideals. Development and experience do not necessarily imply this, so if it is a desirable goal it must fall to the enabling curriculum to promote it. Of course, the emerging set of values and ideals must itself reflect the general value-system within which the curriculum is to operate, which is for present purposes a democratic one, designed to function within the various contexts that have been considered. A curriculum designed to operate within a quite different framework of values might also be termed 'enabling', but if this were to apply where only a forms approach, or a social-imperatives approach, was adopted, then its enablement would be much more limited in scope. It would be less productive, and less democratic, in its interaction with development and experience in general.

Even so, an enabling curriculum envisages two further outcomes. First, it does not simply condition development and experience, within however congenial a context. Based as it is on chosen values, it also enables choices to be made. Choices have to be made in any life situation, and choices made in the light of development and of experience are usually more wisely made than those made, as it were, at random. An enabling curriculum is intended to go beyond this again.

It is intended to reveal more clearly the conditions within which choices have to be made, and the influences which bear upon the chooser. Having stripped off much of the surrounding opacity, it leaves the chooser and the choice face to face. Then, the chooser depends on the emerging set of values and ideals. For it is the ultimate strength, as well as the perversity, of personal autonomy that choices must eventually be made without dictation. In a democratic ideology, autonomy and not automation must be the intention, and the curriculum must enable but not compel. The most that an enabling curriculum can do is to leave the doors and the options open: this it should do, and it is a great deal to do.

Secondly, an enabling curriculum must enable *acceptance*. This may seem to contradict the enablement of choice, but in fact it places choice in perspective. It is not false humility or social quietism, but a recognition that, in our existential situation, individuals must accept limitations, not least in themselves. It sets in perspective the aim often suggested for education, that all children should be enabled (*sic*) to develop their powers to the utmost of which they are capable. For such an aim can be achieved only if it includes the power of acceptance of limitations, constraints, frustrations, disappointments, betrayals, accidents, illnesses, disasters and deaths. It may be unfashionable to emphasise this, but a curriculum that has nothing to say to these experiences, in the face of which development usually also remains silent, is a disabling mockery. Too often, primary education has been envisaged for an unreal world created by wishful-thinking adults who prefer to sweep the unpleasant and the tragic, vicariously, under the carpet while claiming that in doing so they are 'protecting' children. A truly enabling curriculum has to enable those who meet it in the interaction between development and experience to accept reality in all its ugliness as well as all its beauty and potential.

Before the argument is taken further, it would be useful to indicate how this enabling curriculum relates to some terms which are more familiar in discussions of the primary curriculum. One of these is *progressive*. The enabling approach has much in common with the mainstream of progressive education, whose opponents might well assume that it is little more than a variant on that theme. But the usual contention of advocates of progressive education is that it should be more self-consciously linked with children's active learning and also with a mildly socialist orientation generally. The commitment of an enabling approach to forms of understanding might also be viewed with some suspicion. Much the same might be true of the term *child-centred*. An enabling curriculum is intended to be more than child-centred. It takes account also of differences in social situation, and here again the acceptance of forms of understanding may act as a mark of distinction between an enabling and a child-centred approach. At first these distinctions may seem trivial and tedious, but they do in fact embody quite an important distinction between the typical embodiment of educational reformism and what is recommended here. For in the enabling curriculum the process approach has the principal, but not the only, place. In the

## One Approach to Primary Education 51

remainder of this book an attempt will be made to use a consistent terminology about the enabling curriculum, even if it sometimes involves a tendency to be repetitive.

There will certainly be objections to this enabling curriculum, especially perhaps from those who are sincerely convinced of the primacy of forms of understanding and endeavour as such, and of the predominent significance of subjects and disciplines. Almost as many objections could be raised by those who, from whatever point of view, accord first place to social imperatives. There will also be others, of a philosophical cast of mind, who will contend that this enabling curriculum may not in fact do the enabling that is expected of it, and that other types of curriculum might in fact be found to do the enabling at least as well, or even better. They may maintain that it represents just the kind of wishful and soft-centred extrapolation from selected research findings and from edited experience that has plagued English primary education ever since Plowden, modified only by a touch of existentialist pessimism. Still others will cavil at the mixture of forms and process that is advocated, and may wish to substitute something more sturdy and homogeneous; this position might be adopted by Blenkin and Kelly (1981) with their radical empiricist model, or by Egan (1979) with his essentially developmental approach, or by those such as Kirby (1981) who adhere more closely to the child-centred tradition. Much that is advocated in this enabling curriculum corresponds to the central tenets of one or more of these approaches, so that they are more likely to criticise it for lack of clarity and homogeneity—a curricular fudge-and-mudge, an embodiment of Richards's 'liberal pragmatism' (1982, Part 1)—than to regard it as embodying the spirit of reaction. Certainly, it would gain if upheld by empirical verification, which would be a lengthy and complex business. In default of such confirmation, it is presented as a relatively appropriate way of intervening beneficially in the interaction between development and experience. What is more, it tallies with much that Richards (1982, Part 2) calls for in his advocacy of a well-grounded, 'fine-grained' curriculum consistency.

Of course, there may also be misgivings from teachers at the chalk face, who, especially on a wet afternoon when the children are in a silly mood and their colleagues appear indifferent, may be sceptical about anything so smoothly enunciated in words and may—quite rightly—murmur something about the limitations of 'power and constraint' (Taylor *et al.* 1974) that cannot be set aside.

Yet it is just for reality of this kind that an enabling curriculum is envisaged, and I believe that it will survive and prove itself within that reality, even when it is, metaphorically, crumpled and spattered with paint and left pinned on the wall when everyone goes home. For then it really does interact with development and experience to produce an outcome which is moving in the right direction.

I hope that the concept of an enabling curriculum will be seen in that light. In the remainder of this book its nature will be explored, as planned intervention in the interaction between development and experience, together with some of its implications for schools.

## Note

1. The adjective 'enabling' seems more positive than 'facilitating' or 'interactive'. It may even have, as an overtone, the notion of 'ennobling' too. I had come to choose it before I realised that I had heard the term used by the Chief Inspector of Schools Miss Sheila Browne, in an address to the British Association at Liverpool in 1982, before she was appointed Principal of Newnham. It is characteristic of her directness and acumen that she should have coined a term that is at once fresh and apt. I use the same term from now on, with full acknowledgement.

# 5 DEVELOPMENT, EXPERIENCE AND ASPECTS OF THE FORMAL CURRICULUM

The aspects of the curriculum to be considered in this chapter are in one sense an arbitrary selection, though it is unlikely that other selections would deviate greatly from this list. They are not subjects or, necessarily, forms of understanding or endeavour, but rather six elements in children's lives. Here is the list:

Growth, health and movement
Communication
Interpretation of the world
Vision and imagination
Feeling, expression and appreciation
Values and attitudes

The order, like the list itself, is arbitrary but not purely random. It does not imply a hierarchy of difficulty or of importance, nor a developmental sequence. In each aspect development and experience are important, and in each aspect they have been differently investigated by many specialists in that field. Those specialists could each write a book, let alone a chapter, about the theories and research carried out in their own field. As previously indicated, the aim of this chapter is simply to present a brief sketch of each, to bring these sketches together (which is less often done), and to emphasise that all of them are viewed as part of an enabling curriculum. Actual curriculum planning is not included, though Chapter 6 indicates one example of how it might be undertaken.

## Growth, Health and Movement

This is an area that does clearly correspond to an accepted form of understanding and endeavour. At first sight it could be thought of as a simple function of physical development. As children grow older, their bodily growth calls for a response. That is so, but it is only a very limited part of the issue.

First, it is necessary to remember that all aspects of development are related to growth, health and movement. There are processes of intellectual growth too, which are concerned with motor skills and their organisation, while in turn bodily maturation can influence, through the refinement of sensory perception, the formation of concepts. Indeed, the concept of positive health itself is one that has to be learned through what is, in fact, intellectual development. There are also processes of personal/social development which are intimately related to physical growth, in two ways. It is through bodily growth that children acquire the basis for activities which involve social behaviour, and because this growth takes place differently for different children, their relative contributions vary to some extent, so that they are not permanently quite the biggest or the nimblest, though few undergo a total change in their position. Since physical attainments are so evident and so valued as a mark of growth and of status, this sequence has particular significance for personal/social development especially at the primary stage. If in addition we take account of movement and dance and play, the range of significance of physical development in relation to personal development becomes still greater. Finally, the importance of sexual development must be given particular attention since it literally forces itself on the attention of any maker of an enabling curriculum, and is the one aspect of development which requires not merely to be considered when it arises, but also to be anticipated. It is virtually a commonplace of sex education nowadays that it should be introduced factually long before it attains acute personal emotional meaning for individual children, and in view of the trend of sexual maturation, especially in girls, this means in practice starting around the age of 8.

Experience in physical activity is equally important and is given prominence for reasons connected with development itself. If particular forms of physical activity are virtually universal, they are given exercise through forms which belong to particular cultures and communities. Some of these are related to particular aspects of economic life, as when young children learn to paddle canoes or spear fish, but for the most part they are expressions of activity for its own sake. This too may take many forms. It may be co-operative or competitive; it may be limited to one sex or one age-group. Often it takes forms conditioned by the physical environment, for example when climbing or jumping or diving is practised in particular places nearby (Moore, 1984). Sometimes it takes the form of apparently endless experience of particular games, notably football. All of this experience makes its mark on particular children who grow up in any specific place. It also leaves its impression on those who move from place to place, because their experience in general is accumulated from place to place, but added to in dramatic episodes when they encounter new companions in a new place. Even health is affected by experience, since it is possible to be under social pressure to undertake activities which are positive for health, such as swimming, and also others which are negative for health, such as smoking and drug-taking, not to mention the impact of sheer poverty. In a sense the experience of health is particularly elusive, since it is difficult to conceive of health beyond one's experience. (It is of course only too possible to conceive of health that has been lost through injury, disease or other cause, but that is a different matter.) It is possible to go further, as Arnold (1979) does, and to erect a whole philosophy of movement education in which reflective experience is given the special significance associated with phenomenology. But in any view of experience it occupies a central role.

Therefore, any enabling curriculum in physical and health education must take its interaction with development as a starting-point. The planned experience that curriculum constitutes can then be organised in several ways. One is to stake out a set of broad motor skills and prescribe a sequence for each, rather as Pestalozzi did in a very tentative way when trying to draw up an 'ABC' of 'form' to parallel those of language and number[1]. By allowing some adjustment to individual circumstances of development and experience, this can equip teachers and pupils with a repertoire. Toward the opposite end of the spectrum is the essentially developmental approach which has characterised official policy in England and Wales since the middle of the century. The latter seems nearer to the requirements of an enabling curriculum. This can be combined with quite a definable set of attainments, so that assessment is not a major problem. It may present problems of class organisation and control; that is another, though important, issue.

Alongside the active, psychomotor aspects of growth, health and movement, there must also figure a carefully contrived programme of health education and sex education that steers between the sensational and the humdrum, and between the self-centred and the unconcerned. The essential point to bear in mind here is that in any curriculum this element is one with particularly strong overtones in personal experience and social interaction, one too in which individual needs are peculiarly important to cater for, if the other aspects of curriculum are not to suffer as a consequence. These issues are well handled in the Schools Council Project *Health Education 5–13*.

## Communication

As Barnes (1976) reminds us, the basis of any curriculum is communication. Moreover, one of the distinguishing marks of human development is that means of communication are based on physical development, especially in the sensori-motor domain, and are closely linked with intellectual and personal/social development. It is necessary to remember only the vast literature devoted to the origins of human speech and language to appreciate this.

Speech and language constitute only one of the codes of communication that human beings use. Another is number, viewed as a culture-free system of symbols which permits the growth of mathematical skills and of scientific procedures, and thus leads towards two of the widely accepted forms of understanding. Beyond this again are other symbolic media, ranging from body language, facial expression and gesture, through other forms of non-verbal communication such as art and music, to codes that are only now beginning to emerge from the potentialities of electronic and computer technology.

The relation of these modes of communication to development and experience is fascinating. Body language, if we take this first, is quite clearly rooted in development and is the total communication system of the newly-born. Whether speech and language are themselves partly based on innate maturational powers, or whether they depend on development only in respect of vocal capacity, is one of the many issues that can only be mentioned here, though of course it is in itself a major question. As for number, it is generally assumed that the attainment of number concepts is dependent on general intellectual development, but not that the actual language or number arises from any specific aspect of development, or depends on any specific aspect of development. Languages such as art and music raise a whole series of other questions which will later require further comment in relation to aesthetic development, but it is noteworthy that here too there is a general impression that developmental considerations such as neuro-muscular co-ordination and intellectual and emotional growth do matter, but also some variety of opinion about whether there are built-in languages that lead to communication in child art and its musical counterpart.

Whatever may be the variety of views about development in relation to communication, there is general agreement about the decisive importance of experience. In fact, communicating is itself an important form of experience. It is necessary to experience communication before one can communicate experience, though thereafter the two processes are interwoven. Experience powerfully affects speech and language, leaving its mark on every aspect of linguistic behaviour. As regards speech, it is possible to tell not only the country, but even the district of origin of almost any child from how he or she speaks, and this is almost entirely acquired through imitation in the course of experience. It is interestingly linked with development in one important respect that affects primary education, for it is demonstrable that younger children can alter their speech more readily than older children or adolescents or adults. Shaw's *Pygmalion* enjoys some artistic licence; if Eliza Doolittle had been a flower-girl of the tender years familiar in Victorian ballads, then Professor Higgins would have boasted a less preposterous achievement. But the capacity to speak more and more languages correctly in all respects except that of fine intonation does not seem to be tied to developmental stages.

For speech as communication there are other considerations, and these are discussed in many standard works. Psychological studies by such diverse authors such as Vygotsky (1962) and Wartella (1979) are supplemented by sociological investigations such as those conducted by Bernstein and his associates[2]. The general conclusions emerging from all of this work emphasise the importance of parent-child interaction and, to a lesser extent, community circumstances and the influence of the media among the various kinds of experience that affect language development. Written language, and foreign languages, are further extensions of communication which are affected by experience in different social groups.

Number development can also be influenced by experience through the presence of number phenomena in the children's activities and in the environment generally. The presence of significant numbers both cardinal (number of goals scored) and ordinal (bus route No. 5) can have an effect, formerly more unevenly distributed than now, for farm families and some ethnic groups were less accustomed to daily use of number; but in this respect a cultural uniformity has emerged which leaves less room for variety than formerly. Meanwhile, when children are themselves engaged in number-related activities such as buying at shops or stalls, and even more so, selling, then an early acquisition of facility in a limited range of operations is not unusual.

Experience in the languages of art and music is also important. Whatever controversy may hang over the innate capacity of children to communicate in these ways, and about its change as they grow older, there is no doubt that the content of such communication is derived in part from experience, so that here too it is necessary to experience communication before communicating experience. The same is true of body language, and of non-verbal communication generally, whose importance has recently received more recognition[3]. Children's peer society is characterised by the learning from experience of signals of approval and disapproval, challenge and acceptance, which must be understood in order to gain admission to the society, but which are constantly superseded by other codes appropriate to older children. Thus, here there is a sequence of experience related to social development.

There is no aspect of the primary curriculum in which its enabling role is more evident, or more recognised, than in the case of communication. The major contributions to the learning of language and of number, the 'basic skills' of popular parlance, are all based on various interpretations of the interaction of development with experience. Tough's work on communication skills[4], the familiar introductions to number and to mathematics by writers such as Dienes and Matthews, all look to some version of stages of development in interaction with direct experience. If there is any danger here, it is that this relationship is too closely limited to the early stages of the curriculum. For development and experience are both ongoing processes. Just as the beginning of mastery of language and number must be related to both, so must their later extension[5]. And this underscores the need for this further development to take the form of continuing exercise of skills in relation to meaningful content, as advocated in the Primary Survey (DES, 1978) and emphasised by Blenkin and Kelly (1981) and Southgate *et al.* (1981) among others.

Other aspects of communication are usually much less prominently represented in curriculum. Symbolic systems such as pictorial or graphic representation may receive quite a lot of attention, even at the earliest stages when, for example, symbols are used to represent the daily weather, or when the international symbols for road behaviour are learned. Various methods are used to introduce children to musical notation, though it is arguable whether this is the same as providing a mode of communication, even if music itself does. What is true of music is still more true of art, though perhaps less so of craft. As for non-verbal communication, curricular intervention often shows an interesting ambiguity. It is approved and stylised in movement and mime, and may even have what Laban (1948) attempted to provide, namely a code of its own; yet it is related to a vivid peer-language which children normally contrive to keep away from the curriculum. There is thus a dilemma for a teacher wishing to help a newcomer, or a child slow in social development, to understand the code. One possible form of enabling curricular intervention here is to divert attention to references in a story to non-verbal communication among children and adults in other situations, hoping that there will be some facilitation of transfer of understanding to the child's own world.

The final aspect of communication to be mentioned is that of new symbolic systems based on modern technology. Partly these depend, or will depend, on retrieval systems delivering information in various forms. Partly they will come to depend on handling the data from these sources and creating new ideas. This could involve not merely computer languages but also new computer-assisted forms of skill, such as graphicacy. There could even be some by-passing of language and number codes by computerised means, or by direct transmission of bodily messages by-passing to some extent the sense organs themselves. None of these technological possibilities should be excluded from a discussion of communication in the curriculum, but it would be foolish to speculate too far about them. What is quite evident is that they are remote from developmental considerations, and depend on new and at present imperfectly conceived forms of experience. For the present, the basic skills, if strenuously and intelligently handled, remain central to any curriculum designed on process lines. But in a curriculum of this kind, they must be in continuous interaction with development and experience.

**Interpretation of the World**

In one meaning of the phrase, interpretation of the world seems a preposterous element to include in a primary curriculum. In another sense, it is substantially justified. For, as has been indicated in Chapter 2, every child constructs, to some extent, his own experience, his own reality, his own world. The Piagetian processes of assimilation and accommodation and de-centering are means of coming to terms with the external world, something in the same way that Freud saw the transition from fantasy to reality.

There is a sense in which a child's own body and means of communication themselves come to be, in a way, part of the external world. Startling though this may appear, even heredity can be perceived as part of environment in the sense that the general rules belong to the order of nature, and that the individual ego has to come to terms with them. Much the same applies to the development of feeling and expression and appreciation, since these come to be focused on external phenomena, and even to moral values and attitudes as they become less egocentric. But the objective world beyond the child's own body is not merely a focus for communication or feeling or behaviour. It is also something that has to be sorted out intellectually. What has to be clarified is both a set of percepts and a set of concepts. The interaction of development with experience leads to the building up of a store of percepts. The interaction of development with reflection on experience and on the construction and reconstruction of experience leads to the formulation of a succession of interpretations of the world, each appropriate to a stage of development, and each liable to be discarded when new development or new experience renders it inadequate. Herbart, Dewey, Piaget and Bruner would all agree about this. But it is important to realise that the revaluation of these interpretations is not simply the outcome of experience. It does depend in part on development which provides newer and finer tools for the analysis of experience.

It is necessary also to bear in mind that the interpretation of the world is related, pragmatically, to two broad areas of study. The first is what is usually called 'science', that is, the ordering and comprehension of the physical and biological world other than man, or even including man as an organism, in which case it is closely linked with growth, health and movement. This is by common consent one of the basic forms of understanding. The other is known variously as humanities, social studies, social subjects, history-and-geography or (less distinctively) environmental studies, since this implies also some 'science' and this one is uneasily distributed across two or three 'forms'—history, science, social science (if it is separate) and even literature. In practice, the use of the noun 'science' to denote a broad area of subject-matter is misleadingly ambiguous, since it refers to a way of learning and finding out rather than any description of what is learned or found out. It is just as appropriate as a tool in social studies as in what is usually termed science. The real distinction between the two aspects is, of course, that one is concerned with human society and the other is not. Since in this case we have an aspect of curriculum that is closely linked with positive knowledge, both will be briefly considered now, and one of them more fully in the next chapter.

Most of the systematic investigations of children's learning about the objective world have been concerned with 'science' in the usual sense. Piaget and his followers in particular have looked at how children construct schemata for the formulation of explanations, and in a sense it is easier to conduct such investigations with nonhuman than with human phenomena, if only because it is easier to isolate the particular aspects one wants to study. Piaget's untiring enquiries are now widely known and criticised (e.g. Donaldson, 1978). It is largely from these that his formulation of states of intellectual development is derived, and it is largely in relation to 'science' and mathematics that these stages are most directly relevant. Other investigators have suggested amendments, for a number of reasons, in the basic sequence, and have indicated its relation to physical and personal/social development, but nobody working within the 'process' tradition has radically questioned Piaget's approach to cognitive development in relation to understanding of this kind.

The role of experience is implicit in the nature of such learning. It is in encounters with the external world itself that the developmental processes manifest themselves. There is scope for much debate about the sequence of mental operations involved: how far, for example, has the mind to develop before it can select percepts from experience and formulate explanations in terms of concepts? But nobody disputes the need for appropriate experiences, or the consequences when those experiences are lacking.

If we turn to the social-studies aspect of the interpretation of the world, the situation is somewhat different. There have been extensive attempts to delineate sequences in development parallel to those relating to the non-human world, and some parallels are discernible, but in general the new kinds of reasoning and the re-formulation of schemata of explanation come later in chronological age than is the case in reasoning about non-human phenomena. At the same time personal/social development becomes more prominent: learning about society is closely related to living in society. Experience figures also in a rather different guise. It is not just accumulated from finding things in backyards or hedgerows or on television or even in bodily phenomena. That is part of it, but there is also the experience that arises through personal encounter with other people involving communication. There is thus a greater complexity of experience and a different kind of emotional response to it. In the case of pets, this may carry over in some measure into the non-human sphere too, but that does not affect the validity of the distinction.

Thus, it is possible, from development and experience alone, to maintain that the interpretation of the world is of two interrelated kinds. When curriculum endorses this by its division into science and social studies (or whatever term is preferred), that division is thus not a mere echo of academic disciplines. Indeed, it is not very closely related to those disciplines. It does have more in common with a 'forms' approach to curriculum, but is not valid solely on that account. A process curriculum also recognises it in its own right. Only a form of social-imperatives approach could claim to run contrary to it, for example on the grounds that 'science' is necessary at the primary stage as a foundation for the later training of technicians, while social studies are at best superfluous and at worst subversive in the curricular diet for younger children. That view obviously cannot be upheld in relation to an enabling curriculum.

At the same time it is worth while to re-emphasise that the existence of two valid and necessary aspects of the interpretation of the world in formal education at the primary stage does not imply that the two need to be separately taught. What matters is that both should figure, consistently, in the planning of an enabling curriculum for any children aged from 5 to 11, 12 or 13. Within that programme there is a place for topics that include both (and more) of these; for the youngest children, that is almost taken for granted. For older children too it is necessary to show the interrelation between different curricular elements as well as their separate importance.

There are many examples of systematic, enabling curricular intervention in development and experience in 'science'. The Schools Council project *Science 5–13* is the clearest instance in English education, though not the only one, and is notable for actually basing its approach explicitly on the Piagetian stages, though the attempt to combine these with a framework of objectives may have been more problematic (Ennever *et al.*, 1972). Almost inevitably, it was obliged to identify the scientific strand in children's thinking with the teaching of 'science', though its wider implications were made evident. However, as an instance of enabling curriculum design in 'science', it is probably unsurpassed.

There are also instances of enabling curriculum in social studies which take similar account of development and experience. These will be briefly considered in Chapter 6.

**Vision and Imagination**

To leave the question of the interpretation of the world as just a question of positive knowledge, as in the preceding section, is to ignore the other aspects of children's life which are intertwined with it. One of these, not specifically associated with any one form of understanding or endeavour or indeed with any specific kind of process, concerns the extension of horizons involved in vision and imagination. For, alongside the world as it seems to be, there is the world as it might be, and other worlds too. Without vision and imagination, there is no adequate basis for the development of values and attitudes and a conception of what the world should be.

The link between the development of intelligence and knowledge and the role of imagination has attracted attention throughout the ages. The Greek philosophers were aware of both the potentialities and the dangers of imagination. For long it was suspected of engendering falsehood unless duly disciplined. Later, writers such as Froebel regarded imagination with some reverence, as a source of inner life and illumination, displayed in particular in children's play. Montessori viewed this with suspicion, and distinguished between fantasy and the kind of constructive imagination that could be used to amplify knowledge of the real world. Dewey adopted a similar position, though for somewhat different reasons. Meanwhile, Freud's interpretation of the role of fantasy in early childhood and of its relation to the principle of reality, introduced a whole new dimension into ideas about the development of imagination. Thus, the belief that imagination is related to development has a long ancestry, one that is followed by a number of recent writers. One of these, mentioned for the unusual nature of her contribution, is

Cobb (1977), who links childhood imagination with creative evolution and leaves no doubt about her belief in the innate component of imagination. The whole issue is constructively discussed by Sutherland (1971) in her comprehensive analysis of imagination in education. As for vision, it is a slightly precious term and has not received the same close attention as imagination, but it deserves separate naming as a more comprehensive and action-determining element than imagination.

A quite different question is raised when individual differences are concerned. Just as some children are described as 'intelligent', others are looked upon as 'imaginative'. In both cases the real meaning is that they are more so than others. In the case of intelligence the bottom end of the distribution shows a clear relationship with certain pathological conditions. With imagination it is less easy to be sure. There are tests of creativity[6], but that is not quite the same. Imagination is difficult either to detect or to quantify. It is best regarded as a set of qualities which may be manifested by individuals in various ways and to varying extents, at different times, rather than a unitary trait. Then the question of development is side-stepped as regards individuals, and the child's imagination remains largely his own secret, as perhaps it should be.

The relation of vision and imagination to experience is one that raised further far-reaching questions. For it involves the manner and extent of how an individual mind handles and re-shapes and extends what it absorbs or encounters: the very choice of words itself begs a handful of other questions. On the whole, theories based on experience have been less inclined to emphasise imagination than theories based on development, and to those in the Utilitarian or Marxist traditions, imagination can be a positive hindrance. Few, however, would deny that there is some kind of relationship between imagination and experience. Few would then deny that there are qualitative and even quantitative differences in experience between different individuals and groups. Interacting with the observed differences between 'imaginative' and 'prosaic' children—if that is the opposite term—these group and situational differences affect the mental activity of children as we see them.

A word must be added, however abrupt its introduction may appear, about the effects of drugs. It was perhaps at one time unnecessary to mention drugs even in writing about adolescents. Now it is impossible to omit this reference when considering children even of primary age. Whether they have any permanent effect on imagination, or are the cause only of temporary hallucinations, is something to which clinical studies can offer an answer. But psychedelic experience is a mode to which some may resort in sheer despair, one which temporarily suspends some of the consequences of normal experience and even of development. It may also engender visions of a sort. On this issue, which many would prefer to evade, it is impossible not to make a value-judgement. Recognising the social pressures involved, I am still bound to say that experience with drugs is wrong; wrong on Dewey's criterion that it tends to constrict further experience rather than extend it; wrong on developmental grounds because it does not conform to normal growth; and wrong on religious grounds because it arouses a false vision.

Therefore, it is clear that in the case of imagination there are respects in which curriculum has to intervene negatively in the relation between development and experience. However, an enabling curriculum has to occupy a much more positive role too. It has to extend and enrich imagination, and this involves providing activities and curricular experiences which have been found appropriate for this purpose.

The first such medium of nourishment, familiar to educators of young children at least since Froebel's time, is play. Generations of nursery and infant teachers in England have been introduced to its value; elsewhere, the very term kindergarten teacher is a reminder of this approach. Basically it involves providing opportunities for play that are appropriate to development and to the extension of experience. These opportunities are altered as children grow older, and they may include some stimulus to physical, intellectual and aesthetic and moral development too, but in spite of the debasements and caricatures to which the 'play way' has been subjected, it remains in essence play in its own right, as a stimulus to expanding imagination, and only secondarily an introduction to the rest of the curriculum. One error among its advocates has been to neglect to realise that other aspects require other forms of stimulus. Another has been to identify play with games, on the grounds that games serve physical and social development. It is possible, and indeed more usual than is sometimes realised, for children to hate games, even (or especially) games organised by children themselves. But it is by definition impossible for children unless they are deeply disturbed or very handicapped physically to hate play, because play is what it is that they enjoy doing. The art of an enabling curriculum in relation to play, at any age, is to envisage what they may like to do next which will extend imagination and vision as well as enjoyment.

Another medium that has long been recognised as valuable is story. From the earliest years, story can enlarge imagination and vision. It has to take children as they are, so that this in particular is related to individuals and situations. Leila Berg realised this when she saw the inadequacy of middle-class stories for working-class children[7]. However, the growth of imagination is not to be confined to the reflection of environment. Much of the value of story is to illuminate other environments, past, present, future, and outside the world of reality altogether. Stories may embody age-old themes akin to Jung's archetypes, in which case they have a universal appeal and can claim inclusion in curriculum in their own right. They may, however, be quite specific, related to particular interests. For this purpose it is necessary to bridge the gap from stories told to children together, to sufficient mastery of reading to be able to read individually. In an enabling curriculum, this in turn involves a policy of nourishing individual children with a diet of reading, and it is encouraging how many teachers do this, and how many adults, looking back, attribute some aspect of their own growth to the choice of reading offered to them by a percipient teacher. This involves also the need to cater for the less capable readers, and those with visual handicap.

Poetry and descriptive writing are other forms of curricular experience that can be linked with story, for this purpose. So, more strikingly, is drama, which involves group participation and activity and is thus related closely to personal/social development. Drama is particularly appropriate, since so much of children's own experience comes, as was indicated in Chapter 2, in irregular, episodic, dramatic form. Expressive movement provides a further ready mode for imaginative activity in a socially accepted framework. Taken together, and in combination with the experience of art and music to be considered in the following section, this represents a diet that can foster individual imagination perceptively and effectively.

However, the actual course taken by imagination and the formulation of any kind of vision is not predictable. Often it is something that children want to, and have to, keep private. In school they may go through the motions of displaying imaginative behaviour to satisfy the teacher, the group, or the adult world; yet at the same time they may be building up genuine imaginative experience that relates not only to feeling, expression and appreciation, which we shall consider next, but also to values and attitudes and to the formation of a self-concept and, indeed, a self.

## Feeling, Expression and Appreciation

To speak of feeling, expression and appreciation together is to claim that there is an aspect of children's lives which is, broadly, aesthetic in character. This corresponds to another of the usually recognised forms of understanding and endeavour. To introduce this category into the present discussion implies too that development and experience both play a part in its emergence.

This is often assumed nowadays, but it was not always so. The emphasis in, for example, the eighteenth century was often to the effect that such things were impediments to development, and especially to intellectual development, rather than part of it. The Romantic movement reinstated the claims of feeling and expression, and thus in turn drew attention to their place in child development as a valid and legitimate aspect. More recently, and particularly during the early twentieth century, there was rather too much emphasis on it. Almost as though the tables had been turned, it was sometimes maintained, under the impact of psychoanalysis, that intellectual development must be curbed in order not to impair the development of feeling and expression. In all of this the third term, appreciation, occupied a more equivocal position. For it involves a kind of learning, a knowledge about what has been felt by others, together with a maturing capacity to judge for oneself. If aesthetic development is subordinated to intellectual growth, then appreciation may become sterile, a matter of learning about other people's tastes. If the values are reversed, then appreciation can degenerate into the purely solipsistic. Thus, the attitude to appreciation, more even than to feeling and expression, is an index of the position enjoyed by the aesthetic element in any theory of development. Gentle (1981; 1983) has indicated sensitively how the various elements in the development of aesthetic understanding can figure within art education.

Among art educators there has also been a move away from the tendency to claim that aesthetic development is *sui generis* and unrelated to other aspects of development. The notion of broad stages has been worked out here also, but not so directly from the Piagetian model as in some other aspects of development. For example, the notion of artistic development evolved by Viktor Lowenfeld (Lowenfeld and Brittain, 1982), with its stages of scribbling (2-4), pre-schematic representation (4-7), schematic representation (7-9), 'gang-age' realism (9-12), 'pseudo-naturalism' (12-14) and other stages within adolescence, is derived from an observational basis within art education itself, rather than from experiment and interview.

Something similar is to be found in the development of auditory response and discrimination. However, an interesting and important distinction may exist between development in relation to sound as such, and development in relation to music. For the work of pioneers such as Carl Orff, Zoltán Kodály and Justine Ward has emphasised the importance of a sequence of planned experiences in music education, rather than of developmental stages as such. It is significant that a recent piece of research by Alston (1979) has reiterated the importance of an invariant sequence of planned concept-formation, rather than of a developmental process, in the building up of pitch, rhythm, form and harmony as components in aesthetic understanding and endeavour. It could be that there are responses to, and imitations of, the nuances and qualities of sound which do conform to a developmental sequence, but that these are in practice habitually overlaid by the learned, and usually taught, structures of some kind of music, since some kind of music is virtually universal in human cultures. It might be relevant here to note that those contributors to developmental theory such as Froebel who have laid great stress on innate patterns of growth, have nevertheless designated music as an appropriate form of input from teachers, a means of 'making the outer inner', one that would evoke a resonance in the growing child, rather than something that welled up from within.

It then becomes interesting to speculate whether there may be a genuine distinction here between development in respect of understanding and endeavour in visual art and development in respect of understanding and endeavour in music, and if so, where other kinds of aesthetic activity, such as dance and poetry, stand in relationship to art and craft and music in this respect. Understandably, teachers have been more concerned with the total practice of aesthetic education, or indeed of education as a whole, than with the separating out of the relative contributions of development and of experience to aesthetic understanding and endeavour. Nevertheless, this is a consideration which merits attention from those with particular knowledge and experience in this aspect of primary education. As an amateur speculator in this special field, I shall welcome and acknowledge the opinions of experts on the relative contributions of development, as distinct from curricular experience, to different kinds of aesthetic activity among young children.

Looking more closely at the three terms in this section separately, it becomes clear that *feeling* is closely related to physical development. It is partly neurological and thus dependent on the development of the organism. But it is also partly a matter of response, feeling *about* something, or somebody, including feelings about their physical attractiveness or repulsiveness and about how they respond to the child's own feelings in turn. In this sense it is closely related to social development and in particular to relations within the family. There are feelings about smoothness or sliminess that arise directly from perception through touch, and others about sounds or smells that are of similar origin. Emotions may be aroused by the tolling of a bell, the first sight of the sea, or the sensation of sliding down a chute. But in most cases the development of these feelings is closely related to people.

*Expression*, unlike feeling, is an activity. Feeling may give rise to it; physical development may circumscribe it. To judge from children's apparently spontaneous singing, skipping, or even drawing, the beginnings of expression seem to arise largely as a part of development. Moreover, the urge to express something seems to follow patterns which are related to general growth. As languages of communication come to be mastered, new avenues of expression are opened: this is particularly true of forms of verbal and written expression. If these are developmentally influenced, then they are not entirely dependent on any particular stimulus.

*Appreciation* is more difficult to infer. It appears that preferences, even strong preferences, for different kinds of aesthetic experience do arise independently of specific experiences. Whether these are related solely to conditioning, or whether they are a response to something personal, unique and innate, must remain a matter for debate. Generally, however, there is a developmental pattern, which enables stages such as Lowenfeld's to be demarcated.

When we turn to consider the ways in which feeling, expression and appreciation relate to experience, the perspective becomes different. Feeling and expression are both responses to experience, and the more vivid and striking the experience is at the stage the child has reached, the more intense the feeling is likely to be. It is not so certain that the expression will be equally intense or apparent. Sometimes it is consciously or unconsciously evaded or held back, or conveyed obliquely, as when a child's deep but unconscious resentment at a bereavement results in savagely drawn pictures of armed combat. However, any curriculum that gives due place to aesthetic behaviour is bound to take account of the relationship between experience and this aspect of a child's life. In feeling and expression, the interaction of development with experience is perhaps seen at its clearest.

With appreciation, this is less clear. Cultural and subcultural factors are at work, indicating to children what they should, and should not, like. This does not imply total submission to cultural control, but there is considerable evidence that cultural influences are powerful both in determining what visual, musical or other experiences children are exposed to, and how they are expected to respond. A boy of 10 in a working-class district is more likely to respond to what he sees as beauty in a goalkeeper's save than to what he might see as beauty in a sunset. But a sunset can still surprise him.

The intervention of an enabling curriculum into this kind of interaction is a particularly delicate matter. This is not because there is anything precious about it, or about this aspect of children's lives. Their tough resilience can be seen, for example, in their response to poems about the savagery of wild life. The delicacy arises largely from the very complexity of the issues. To begin with, there is a difference between feeling and experience in education and the place of the Arts in education, for the Arts have an intellectual component too. If we consider first children's feeling and expression, then clearly this kind of development and experience is peculiarly personal and private, so that it stands at the opposite pole from the palpable aspects of bodily growth and the culturally prominent and safely channelled forms of development such as language acquisition. Yet if we turn to the place of the Arts in education, with its intellectual component, confusion still arises because of the diversity and lack of tight logical sequence that aesthetic education manifests. Faced with this complexity, teachers of younger children usually seem to settle for some workable sequence that is available, linking it with general development in a reasonably consistent way. They frequently incorporate 'creative writing' somewhere in the scheme of things when writing becomes possible, hoping that there will be something to be creative about. They follow one method or another of introducing children to musical intervals and notation as well as to experiments with sound, following this with the enjoyment of singing and perhaps of instrumental music ancient and modern. They introduce, maybe, some stimulus that can lead to expressive dance and movement. In all of this they endeavour to develop appreciation through suitable praise, and through the discussion of examples they regard as in some way good.

This may sound like an unkind caricature. In fact, it is quite an achievement to do as much as this, consistently, over the primary years, taking account of developmental progression from gross-motor to fine skills, from simple to more complex tools, from individual to paired and group work, and from topics suited to infants to those adapted to the threshold of adolescence. A response to development and experience on these lines permits also the progressive fostering of a sense of unity, wholeness, and rightness in activities and products of increasing complexity and sophistication that can be systematically assessed along the lines suggested by Eisner (1972) and others. In some ways this is the most challenging and demanding part of any primary curriculum, if not the first to appeal to cost-conscious politicians, yet it can be the most impressively rewarding, not only in its own terms but in its significance as curricular experience for general educational development. This is a phenomenon that can often be observed in Special Education, where proportionately more attention is paid to feeling, expression and appreciation in the curriculum.

**Values and Attitudes**

Even more than communication, values are essential to human living. Attitudes are in a sense the expression of values. A curriculum that aims to enable choice and acceptance must be concerned in particular with values and attitudes, and with the moral and religious forms of understanding which they embody.

If a totally naturalist view of human nature were valid, then all values and attitudes would arise developmentally. The seeds of virtue would be implanted in every child, and desirable values would emerge spontaneously and grow as part of maturation. It might even be possible to envisage the reverse of this process, in which children are actually born with more virtue than they have later when shades of the prison-house close about them. Wordsworth was not the only writer to have expressed this belief. But this is not a view that can be seriously sustained. Not only does it deviate from observed reality; it is also an instance of the naturalistic fallacy through which it is inferred that what things are, they ought to be. So in this sense the development of values and attitudes, unassisted, is an absurdity.

In another sense it is however a necessity. If instead of trying to deduce values from development, attention is paid to how values generally seem to develop, then this is open to observation. To some extent, values are related to physical development. Even during childhood sexual maturation begins to demand some revaluation of assumptions, though opinions may differ about how widely this change affects values and attitudes in general, and how sex-differences influence perceptions of equality. Piaget was quick to grasp the relationship between the decline of egocentricity in intellectual operations and the decline of egocentricity in what is seen as valuable in life. Studies of political and social values display a developmental pattern similar to the development of mathematical and scientific thinking, though on a rather longer time-scale.

Prominent among considerations of the development of values and attitudes, and rightly so, is moral development. Educators have always regarded moral values and attitudes, the determinants of personal and social behaviour, as a principal concern. Therefore, it is not surprising that Piaget (1932) detected stages in moral development, or that their modification and extension by Kohlberg[8] and others has been a prominent feature in studies of this kind. Kohlberg's stages of development are now a familiar part of educational discourse. Usually they are presented as six steps, some of which coincide with the span of primary education. These stages move from a stage viewing morality as arbitrary and imposed, through one embodying rules that must be obeyed for fear of punishment, then one which is more related to immediate rewards and satisfactions, next one concerned with social esteem as a 'good boy' or 'nice girl', and finally, beyond what are normally the primary years, to the beginning of an idea of morality closely associated with law and order. Subsequent stages are more open to dispute, but they lie further beyond the scope of primary education. The details of the stages are a matter for discussion and research, as is the means whereby children move developmentally from one stage to the next, and the extent to which the boundary between stages is a rigid one, or one that is quickly traversed. Kohlberg's view is that children can comprehend the reasoning appropriate to one stage, but only one, ahead of their present situation. Despite the controversy to which they have given rise, Kohlberg's stages have gained widespread currency, and it is evident that they can have important significance for both intellectual and personal/social development.

To emphasise the role of experience in relation to values and attitudes is unnecessary. It is a commonplace of social science that they are substantially learned by imitation from the surrounding culture, and that this learning is not merely confined to social mores, but extends also to cognitive styles and even to physical development. And what is true of cultures as a whole applies also to subcultures, so that the generalisations of anthropologists are supplemented by those of sociologists. Studies of child-rearing practices, of community and peer-group processes, indicate the ways in which values and attitudes are acquired, and also how they can be and are modified. The consequences of social mix and of social change are also important; indeed a study such as Riesman's *The Lonely Crowd* (1956) suggests how the mechanisms of learning values and attitudes from experience themselves vary when social structure changes. From the earliest times, world-wide, it has been widely believed that values and attitudes could be improved through experience of deliberate changes in social organisation, and of course this remains a cardinal tenet of at least one major political doctrine today, while to another, namely Dewey's form of democracy, values and attitudes develop and improve through experience itself.

Individual experiences, too, can be decisive, through the warmth of particular relationships or through hostility or trauma or disaster.

On any showing, then, values and attitudes represent a centrally important outcome of experience related to a developmental sequence which, irrespective of its causes, is manifest in children's behaviour. Yet if there is any component of curriculum in which enabling intervention is most imperative, this is it. The means by which such intervention can be contrived is less easy to define. If experience could be conceived in terms of simple conditioning, then Skinner's sophisticated behaviourism would be sufficient. If more importance is attached, as it must be, to the response of the individual child, which also implies allowing more importance to developmental considerations, then there is a case for a planned sequence of moral and social education. This can be pieced together eclectically from a whole series of considerations, including Kohlberg's theory, and is nowadays a subject to which a great deal of new thought is being given. A usual pattern includes the learning of generally accepted rules of social behaviour in the early years, with an increasing learning of individual and collective responsibility for choice, for the making and amending of rules, and for something like the 'considerate style of life' that is the aim of the Schools Council Moral Education 8 – 13 project. (McPhail *et al.*, 1978). Whatever aims moral education may have, it is necessary to translate these into the terms appropriate to the developmental level and experience of the children. Thus, with older juniors fairness is more susceptible of emphasis than equality, and justice than tolerance. Only in a strong social-imperatives approach can an attempt be made to ignore this constraint.

If the means of moral education are difficult to define and dependent on gradualism, its ends are still more problematic. To assume that the operation of a democratic procedure, and even of a considerate life-style, will in itself generate a moral code and the motivation to adhere to it is to make an act of faith in human nature akin to Dewey's, an act that is not rendered defensible simply because it is widely and often inexplicitly assumed by people of demonstrable integrity and goodwill, preoccupied by the dangers of any form of indoctrination. A slightly different stance is that represented by Durkheim[9], who considered that this kind of democratic process required a firm framework of direction and of social control in order to succeed even within the secular openness of the Third Republic in France. In the case of Christian, Islamic or Marxist societies, a still more positive direction is given. This is a point at which the process curriculum is most under strain, and at which the acceptance of a distinctive moral form of understanding does not in itself do more than clear the decks for positive moral growth. Much the same is true of Herbart's construction of a moral agent. Yet if the gap here were to be filled by a social-imperatives approach, the whole case for resisting that approach in the rest of the curriculum would be weakened. No one resolution of this particular issue is likely to gain general acceptance in a plural society, except the recognition that the issue is immensely important; that it is complex; that any answer sought and chosen by individuals, including teachers, will be ultimately derived from outside the curriculum;

and that for these very reasons it is essential to preserve the openness of a society so that no one set of social imperatives is permitted to foreclose the issue for the society as a whole.

The practical problem may in fact be rather less stark than this. For it is possible to combine the point of view just enunciated with what might be termed the positive principle of the lowest common multiple, whereby a core of decent behaviour is distilled from a whole set of available moralities and cumulatively built up during the course of school education. This may include rule-governed behaviour in the classroom and school, the encouragement of sympathy and generosity, and the open discussion of moral choices. At the primary stage this approach can be taken quite a long way, and is indeed widely practised. It does involve some positive guidance, reinforced by democratic consensus, and it constitutes a seedbed within which individual moral growth can be taken much further, as part of the development of personal autonomy that Dearden (1968) regards as fundamentally important, and also of the building up of the emergent self. In practice, this further personal growth is likely to be influenced by contact with others, and particularly with teachers, and it is unrealistic to conceive of a primary education in which this does not happen.

There are, however, two important limitations in this lowest-common-multiple approach. One is that it can only go a part of the way, and thus is not necessarily adequate for continuation into secondary education. More important is that it may be carried out in such a way as to suggest that it is in itself adequate, and that the intensity of interest shown in moral issues by adults who, in Kohlberg's view, are at stages literally beyond the comprehension of young children, is a sign not of moral maturity but of rather quirkish eccentricity, one of the varieties of human nature to be inspected, rather like the succession of impressions conveyed by Mussorgsky in his *Pictures from an Exhibition*. To convey such an impression would be to stultify moral development rather than to encourage it.

In addition to all of this, it may be necessary also to effect specific adjustments to situations in which there are unusual clashes of values through the juxtaposition of socio-economic, ethnic and cultural groups with contrasting values, a point that will be considered more specifically in Chapters 7 and 8. Such circumstances serve as a reminder that development and experience will always continue to exercise a powerful influence alongside curriculum, whatever the school may attempt to do. Ultimately, no school can be an island, or a little monastery or convent, unto itself.

Until now, nothing has been said about religious education. That is deliberate. The development of values and attitudes, and indeed a programme of moral education, is entirely possible without any reference to religious education. But there are three ways in which religious education must be considered.

First, it is still in England a statutory obligation, and in voluntary schools, more than that. Hedged about as it is by conscience clauses, here it has still to be included for reasons quite different from those hitherto advanced. To say this is to do no more than to repeat the obvious, with perhaps an expectation of some suggestions for evading a tiresome anachronism.

The claims of development and of experience do not, in fact, permit such a ready dismissal. Some sort of religious component figures in many general studies of child development, even though it tends to decline in prominence during adolescence. More specifically, the work of Goldman and others[10] has suggested a specific sequence of *religious* development. This is clearly related to experience too: a sequence in a Buddhist society must differ from a sequence in an Islamic society, and both, from Goldman's English scene. However, within any one context there does appear to be a developmental pattern, and substantial experience of religious institutions, and curricular intervention has in recent years been shaped to take this into account much more than previously, in primary education (e.g. Dean, 1971) as well as in secondary education.

None of this fully faces the challenge of religious belief to be true. If it is, in the faith of a teacher or a parent, then the question of values and attitudes must be a function of that belief. If it is not true, in the opinion of a teacher or a parent, then the question of values and attitudes must be answered accordingly. In a plural society, then, it is important to recognise that different values and attitudes and beliefs are strongly held by other people, and that children have to construct their own, just as they have to construct their own experience. This being so, it is necessary to face here, as in the case of moral education, and even more so, the danger of the *Pictures from an Exhibition* approach. For the adherents of one faith, it is tempting to present all others in this implicitly devaluing context while asserting the truth of their own. For the adherents of no faith, it is necessary only to go one step farther and to present them all in

## Development, Experience and the Formal Curriculum 77

this light. To do either is to misrepresent fundamentally the religious form of understanding, and with it a whole facet of human experience which many believe to be the most important of all. Of course, for those who are constrained to represent one form as true, as I am, it is not enough to present religious experience in all its depth and variety. But it is the first essential step, and the only one that may legitimately be assigned to the curriculum. For a school as such is not, and cannot be, the instrument whereby in an open society with a process curriculum, values are determined. What is true of morality is here equally true of religion. Churches may take a stand, and church schools may succeed in developing a characteristic atmosphere; but ultimately the profession of belief is an individual matter. Schools can do no more than resist the *imposition* of any one set of values, social, political or religious. For any imposed values, even those which are intended to promote toleration, are ultimately false.

### Conclusion: a Unitary Curriculum

Six aspects of an enabling curriculum have now been considered, and one of them will be amplified in the next chapter. None of these aspects is quite the same as a form of understanding or endeavour, still less an area of subject-matter, though all of them can be related to curricular content, and to any way in which curriculum is subdivided for older primary children.

Yet the formal curriculum as a whole should, throughout the primary years and perhaps afterwards, be considered as a unity. The six aspects and their interrelation are present at each stage, and the subdivision of the curriculum into 'content areas' as they are termed in Schools Council Working Paper 55 (Ross *et al.*, 1975) or further into individual subjects, can itself be looked upon as a way of adjusting curriculum so that its intervention in the interaction of development with experience becomes more effective.[12] Yet the unity of the curriculum also serves this purpose, and the task of primary education is to conserve that unity as well as to encourage progressive and meaningful differentiation of skill, knowledge and endeavour. If there is to be discussion about a core curriculum, then this, rather than a sterile subdivision into skills without application and content without purpose, should be the essence of that core.

For each individual it must be what Staines (1977) refers to, though in a somewhat different sense, as a 'self-curriculum'. Its purpose, it will be recalled, is general enablement. Where development interacts with experience, there the curriculum is to intervene positively. It is to equip the child not just with skills and content or even values and attitudes and understanding, but with the capacity to choose and to accept, and in Bruner's terminology, to cope rather than merely to defend (Bruner, 1966). No one-to-one correspondence can be assumed between any aspect of curriculum and these eventual outcomes. The value of the curriculum for each individual must depend on his or her own development and experience, and on the ways in which it influences in its turn the positive nature of development and the beneficial quality of experience. The vindication of such a curriculum can be demonstrated only through a lifetime of development and experience, and only then if it is consummated by ideals and beliefs that lie beyond curriculum.

Meanwhile, it is at least evident that primary education built around a curriculum such as this, must be an intellectually and personally demanding activity for all those who are involved in it. This chapter has indicated only an outline of what is involved, and is sorely in need of detailed correction by those who are experts in the various aspects, as well as by those whose own development and experience in primary education qualifies them to pronounce with authority upon their own field of professional expertise[11]. For we are only now beginning to understand the range of collective wisdom that primary education requires.

### Notes

1. This feature of Pestalozzi's work constituted one part of his attempt to establish a coherent theory of elementary education. If there were to be exercises in the basic desk skills, so there should be in movement. Incidentally, this was the feature of his theory that Herbart selected for criticism in his earliest published work.
2. Much of the recent work of Bernstein and his associates has been concerned with the social context of language acquisition among young children. See the *Class, Codes and Control* series (Routledge & Kegan Paul).
3. For a simple introduction, see Eisenberg, A.M. and Smith, R.R. (1971), *Nonverbal Communication*, Indianapolis, Bobbs-Merrill. Some of the educational implications of nonverbal communication are suggested in W.A.L. Blyth (1976) 'Non-verbal Elements in Education: Some New Perspectives', *British Journal of Educational Studies*, XXIV, 2, 109-26. See also May, Mary R. (1980), *The Relationship of Verbal and Nonverbal Communication*, The Hague, Mouton.
4. Notably in the publications of the Schools Council *Communication Skills Project*, which has been concerned with all ages 3-13. The most significant embodiment of her point of view is probably Tough (1977a).

5. A particularly good discussion of these issues is offered by Hutchcroft (1981).

6. There is a whole literature on creativity and its relation to intelligence and development. One of the most important contributions is that of Wallach, M.A. and Kogan, N. (1965) *Modes of Thinking in Young Children: A Study of the Creativity-Intelligence Distinction*, New York, Holt, Rinehart & Winston.

7. Leila Berg was one of the first authors to attempt to base the literacy of working-class children on themes related deliberately to their environment. See in particular her *Nippers* series (Macmillan): its title is as firmly embedded in its decade as in its class.

8. Lawrence Kohlberg has not embodied his ideas in one definitive volume. A useful introductory survey is to be found in Duska and Whelan (1977).

9. Emile Durkheim's ideas are embodied in his *Moral Education*, translated by E.K. Wilson and H. Schnurer (1961), New York, Free Press. See Chapter 2, note 4 above.

10. Developmental studies in religious understanding are well exemplified by Goldman, R. (1965), *Readiness for Religion*, Routledge & Kegan Paul, especially Part I, chapter 3.

11. Blenkin and Kelly (1983) have recently edited an important sequel to their earlier book (Blenkin and Kelly, 1981), one in which some aspects of the primary curriculum are considered from a 'process' standpoint. Although, as indicated in Chapters 3 and 10, their emphasis differs somewhat from my own, the expert treatment of the various aspects of curriculum in this new volume provides a telling commentary on the present chapter. Since no reference is made to social studies, it does not have comparable relevance to Chapter 6.

12. While this book was in press the Schools Council published a valuable new study entitled *Primary Practice: a Sequel to 'The Practical Curriculum'*, Working Paper 75, Methuen Educational, 1983.

# 6 AN EXAMPLE: THE INTERPRETATION OF THE SOCIAL WORLD

In order to give a little more substance to the general sketch of aspects of the children's world expounded in Chapter 5, attention will now be paid to one area of the primary curriculum, arguably the one that is most closely related to social development and social experience. In Chapter 5 it was introduced as one part of the child's interpretation of the world, the part that is concerned with human society. Because this particular aspect of the children's world is closely linked with positive knowledge and intellectual ordering, as is 'science', it is often considered along with science as a part of the structure of curriculum. For the human element in this interpretation of the world, the title to be accorded to this part of the curriculum is itself problematic. Sometimes it is known as social studies, sometimes as environmental studies (which includes some 'science'), sometimes as humanities, and sometimes it is not specifically known as anything at all, being submerged in topic work or projects or centres of interest. Sometimes, indeed, it is prone to be omitted altogether; but that would not be compatible with the process curriculum under discussion. Here it will be given the designation *Place, Time and Society*, after the Schools Council project of that name[1]. Unlike that project, however, it will be related to the whole curriculum 5-13, as was the Schools Council project *Environmental Studies* which preceded it[2].

The actual title requires elucidation. One major category of the phenomenal world is space. Within this general category 'place' is here used to denote those spatial relationships that are of particular concern to a geographer; the distribution of human phenomena, the patterns which they manifest, and the relations between these patterns. It also involves some skill-mastery in graphicacy (Boardman, 1983) and in map-making and map-reading. So it refers both to the concept of place and to the properties of place-relations. Similarly, 'time' means historical time, and the conventional way of measuring and grouping time, but also some understanding of the past. As for 'society', this is used as a generic term to include the subject-matters of economics, sociology, anthropology, politics and psychology. Obviously, at close quarters, 'society' overlaps 'place' and 'time'. It also differs from them because they have figured in philosophy as fundamental categories, within which 'society' is one of the major phenomena.

It would indeed be possible to halt at this point and spend a long time indicating the depth in which philosophers and social scientists have argued about the three terms in this title and their interrelations. So it is with any other issue in curriculum. The only viable procedure is to recognise this vulnerability, to realise that it is beyond the bounds of practicality to pursue every question as it ideally should be pursued, and for the rest to operate within the conventional limits usually observed by others concerned with educational issues, confident that if a major change, a paradigm shift, as it were, should take place in the ways in which terms such as place, time and society are conventionally handled in the discourse of intelligent and educated people, then this change will be reflected from specialist into generalist discussion, and that it will become evident to anyone who continues to remain intellectually and professionally alive and vigilant.

In considering place, time and society in the primary curriculum, the first step will be to look in more detail at the ways in which development and experience relate to place, time and society in children's lives, and then to consider the possibilities and limitations of curricular intervention at different age-levels from 5 to 13. In the course of this discussion it will become apparent that all the six aspects of curriculum are to some extent involved, though the interpretation of the world is the most prominent of the six.

During the first five years of life, children's first notions of spatial and temporal relations and social organisation take quite substantial shape. Thus, they bring considerable equipment to school with them.

In part this equipment is traceable to development. The growth of sensory powers enables them to make sense of their immediate surroundings; the growth of intellectual powers goes along with and is nourished by contact with things and people; personal/social development itself constitutes a basis for understanding something of adult-child relations and of rudimentary relations between children of the same and of different ages. In broad terms, the Piagetian sequence from sensori-motor, through pre-operational, to intuitive thought, with its progressive reduction in egocentric responses, has clear significance for the ways in which place, time and society are seen. At first few places are perceived, memory is short, the separateness of other people only slowly understood, and organisation of ideas and prediction of consequences rather random and associated with fantasy. Because human affairs are complex, and spatial and temporal concepts difficult, progress in understanding these is rather slower than in relation to material things.

Alongside this evident cognitive growth and its importance for the understanding of the social world, there is the effect of other aspects of development. Already children are aware of their own physical growth and of their growing capacity to achieve in power and agility, so that they begin to formulate some concept of children in society as well as of what adults can, at least in some spheres, do. Some, too, will have begun to achieve sufficient mastery of language to be able to draw, from television and other sources, some idea of the wider world, and may also be embarked on a diet of books about it; but in detail that is rather a matter of experience. Many more will be, by virtue of their stage of cognitive growth, also at a time when imagination and fantasy are intertwined with reality, and when some aspects of their private imagination are in one sense very real, though progressively separable from the objective world. They will have too a power of intense feeling for some persons and some things (which may be personalised) and this will influence their own modes of expression. As for appreciation, that will not yet be formulated. Values and attitudes will be highly specific and changeable, substantially egocentric, but felt to be important. Yet because communication is not yet fully developed, the visibility of the other aspects of development to adults is limited. It is a state of affairs that teachers in reception classes are familiar with, and to which they are often able to react in an almost intuitive manner, which gives them a peculiarly direct relationship with children whose own thinking is largely intuitive.

In all these respects, experience has also already played an important part. The ways in which physical growth are affected by experience are evident. Various urban and rural settings influence the choice of activities that encourage particular skills and powers (Moore, 1984), and in each the actual patterns of activity are powerfully affected by peer influences. But this is more than physical growth. It is part of the local culture, and it embodies something of what children learn, almost incidentally, about the nature of a society as a whole. Meanwhile, before the age of 5, children encounter much variety of cognitive experience, varying from one environment to another, and all increasingly extended through the ready access to the media which is commonly available. Through both immediate and vicarious experience they also come to see more of their own place within society, while everyday interactions enable them to embark upon particular forms of behaviour and to acquire a repertoire of social responses which is already well stocked when they begin school, and which continues to expand in various ways while they are in primary schools (Stevens, 1982).

One particular aspect of this knowledge, to which increasing attention has been given in recent years, is the learning of sex roles. Although the cleavage between the sexes in play and friendship groups has not yet begun to develop strongly, children are already substantially aware of what is expected of girls and boys respectively, and also, though less immediately, of what is expected of women and men respectively. There is a continuing debate about the relative importance of developmental and experiential factors in this respect. However, recently it is the importance of experience that has been emphasised. Toys, books, the message of the media, all of these tend to reinforce what is generally regarded as sex-appropriate behaviour, and frequently also to emphasise specific traits and interests that were not prominent a decade or two ago, or to alter those, such as clothing, which were.

Attention has also come to be focused on learning about ethnic differences. Some of it is distinctly unflattering to teachers. It is thus all the more important to remember that ideas on differences between ethnic groups are often embedded in experience before formal schooling begins. Social class does not appear to figure so closely within early learning from experience, partly because it does not have the same 'visibility' as sex or ethnic differences, but when it is translated into differences in speech habits or syntax, then it may take the form of the strange or unknown and form the basis of two ideas, first, that some people are different, and secondly, that when they are, other people behave in certain ways towards them. Other experiences may draw attention to differences between religious groups or other subdivisions in the locality or more widely. Thus, even in a reception class children are already equipped with considerable unsystematic knowledge of place and society, even if their sense of time and of sequence is rather more rudimentary. It is with this equipment that they first encounter the official social curriculum of the school itself.

This curriculum is usually mapped out in such a way that it can include a systematic introduction to the interpretation of the social world. However, it does not necessarily succeed in effecting that introduction. This may be in part because in the name of progressive education it has sometimes been assumed that teachers need not do more than devise a succession of projects or topics within which appropriate attention would somehow be paid to place, time and society. It is a form of curriculum planning akin to the economic thought of Adam Smith, according to which some invisible hand would ensure overall balance. Any curriculum that takes some note of the major intellectual achievements of mankind, even if it does not refer to 'forms' as such, must be more systematic than this. Bruner's spiral curriculum (1960), for example, presumes that certain fundamental notions about human society should be systematically introduced over the whole course of primary and secondary education. At the same time, the bewildering wealth of possible content and complexity in the social subjects enforces some principles of selection. The approach suggested by the Schools Council project *Place, Time and Society 8−13* is that the emphasis should be on the attainment of skills, concepts and attitudes, and this is an approach that is becoming almost commonplace in England not only in primary education but also in secondary and further education too.

If this is seen as a common programme, then it is possible to suggest a sequence of skill acquisition and of concept and attitude formation that could constitute a standard programme. But if it is seen essentially as intervention in the interaction between development and experience in an enabling curriculum, then the planning becomes a more complex matter. For there is no area of the curriculum in which differences in development and experience are more important than this. All that can be done is to suggest lines on which each school can plan its own programme, steering between rigidity on the one hand and structurelessness on the other.

The first question is how the skills, concept and attitudes important in understanding place, time and society can be related to development and experience in the younger primary years. Often, too modest a view has been taken of the children's powers and interests. Place has been regarded as little more than the ordering of perceptions of the local environment and perhaps some simple recording of weather. Society has implied little more than some basic social education without much reference to learning about society. Time has indeed been assumed beyond the children's experience, except for stories from 'long ago'[3]. If separate studies of these three elements are considered, in isolation from each other and from the rest of the curriculum, then of course this is quite inappropriate for children of 5 or 7, though that consideration has not impeded attempts to do so. If, however, the emphasis is on questions that can be used to extend experience and to build on development, this is not only possible but important. Suppose that a story is told and some movement or painting follows. Teachers are accustomed to using this sequence to accustom children to the relevant vocabulary, and perhaps to encourage imaginative experience. What is needed is a habitual inclusion in the teacher's discourse of these key questions: Where? When? Who? How? and Why?

'Where?' questions of course relate to place. That does not mean that they should be pedantic attempts to recall place names. It is rather a matter of asking 'Where did the boy go to get . . . ?' and 'Where do you go to get . . . ?' thus linking it with experience. From such questions it is possible to ask next 'How can we show where he went . . . ?' and thus introduce the first three-dimensional 'map' and perhaps even a simple sketch. Later on there can be a much more systematic look at place and how it is represented, but these are the first steps. Necessarily, different situations in the children's experience will call for different questions and different answers. That is the part of the curriculum that is specific to each situation. But questions that lead outwards and extend experience are important in every situation. In a sense every school and every teacher can devise an upwards spiral whereby the particular children in that situation have their experience widened, its limitations countered, and its possibilities built on.

The second kind of question asks 'When?' This does not call for a date answer: 'In 1965' or whenever it was. The point of asking 'When?' is to encourage children to seriate events and episodes in the correct order. They may be events in a story or in everyday experience, but a teacher can encourage children to think of them as a sequence. As children grow older, it becomes more meaningful also to refer to 'last year', 'in the winter', or 'before the new houses were finished'. In such ways the idea of 'when' in imaginary situations can be linked with 'when' in experience.

The remaining three questions, 'Who?' 'How?' and 'Why?' are not so straightforward. 'Who?' can initially refer to individual characters in a story or a drama, or even in the class itself. It is a means of emphasising the importance of individual characters. But 'Who?' can also refer to groups and collectives. It can mean 'Which groups of people?' and as such it can draw attention to the existence of groups. It is here that the children's previous experience of groups is important, as well as their stage of development. Some will be more able than others to think of neighbours, friends, even family. Some will be more conscious than others of the distinctiveness of groups, including ethnic groups. All of this reflects experience of the perception of groups, and thus in a sense, all 'Who?' questions imply the question 'Who am I?'

'How?' requires further understanding of social process. Unlike the first three questions, this is not open to a necessary or accurate answer. It may simply call for the best answer that is available. The teacher's own answer must be to some extent a matter of opinion. Within the stylised limits of a story or poem or drama, there may be a 'right' answer—'How the Manx cat lost his tail'—because one explanation, and one only, is part of the story. But when 'How?' questions are translated into terms of everyday life—'How do we get our milk?'—the answers are of a different order, though still closely linked to individuals' development and experience.

The final question is 'Why?' It is of course a question that the children themselves constantly ask, and again there are 'Why?' questions about stories that have clear answers within the stories themselves: 'Why did Paddington Bear wear a label?' But as soon as 'Why?' questions begin to apply to everyday life, they are even more difficult to be sure about than 'How?' questions. They may be quite beyond the children's cognitive development, and they may also require knowledge and skills outside their experience. They may also be open to a variety of answers even at the adult level. 'Why has the corner shop closed?'

Of course, place, time and society can figure in the programme for young schoolchildren in other and more positive ways. They may go out and look systematically at their physical and social environment and follow this up with expressive work. They may look at a particular old house or write to a particular school somewhere else, or follow a particularly suitable television programme or series. Work of this kind, if adjusted to general development and experience, is valuable, and children can often do more of it than is expected of them. But the five questions give some consistency and coherence to the kind of thinking that is necessary to understand society. They are five pointers to place, time and society that can be introduced from the very start, and can constitute good study habits for the future.

Beyond the age of, say, 7, a more systematic approach to place, time and society becomes possible. The skills, concepts and attitudes central to this area of the curriculum can be more specifically identified and fostered, against a background of further development and widening experience. These skills, concepts and attitudes follow directly on the five questions. They overlap quite substantially what is taking place in the rest of the curriculum, but this area of knowledge of human affairs has a distinctive emphasis of its own. The brief suggestions that follow are adapted from objectives initially designed for *Place, Time and Society 8–13* itself.

There is first a set of instrumental skills that require an adequate cognitive base, but are not themselves higher-order cognitive skills. They include knowing how to find and use information, how to set it out in verbal and graphical form, how to make and use maps, how to handle the conventional time scale, even how to handle simple social statistics. Whatever programme a particular school devises, it must include the progressive acquisition of these skills. Immediately it is apparent that this process depends partly on development but more so on experience. To some children such matters are part of their everyday environment. To most they are not, and to them it may appear provocative, frustrating or ridiculous that there are some children to whom they are. This can involve an element of conflict, no more so than in respect of similar skills in the rest of the curriculum, but important nevertheless.

There are, however, cognitive skills which are much more demanding and more specific to place, time and society. Together, they can be termed 'critical thinking skills'. They include the making of hypotheses, the drawing up of generalisations, and the readiness to tolerate uncertainty in explanation—the realisation that 'How?' and 'Why?' questions may be incapable of definite answers. They entail also the understanding of methodological concepts: similarity/difference, continuity/change, causes and consequences. Whatever subject-matter may be chosen in place, time and society, it must allow for the progressive cultivation of these skills, which are themselves an essential feature of an enabling curriculum that fosters choice and acceptance. They require quite a different procedure from the docile and diligent reproduction of illustrations and distillation of book resources that is sometimes found. They need a readiness to understand issues and to formulate and tackle problems. They depend upon adequate development. The use of hypotheses even of a simple kind is not easy before the stage of concrete operations is reached and, as was indicated in Chapter 5, in this area of the curriculum that is usually reached later than in scientific and mathematical thinking. They also depend on experience, and here again there is great variety. Most children do make hypotheses and generalisations in their everyday lives, but these may be more restricted than is required in the curriculum. As for the tolerance of uncertainty, this may actually be excluded from everyday thinking, though that may well be a strong reason for including it in the curriculum. All of these features of everyday life may differ sharply from one situation to another. In some homes and some peer groups, critical thinking skills of the usual kind may be familiar; in others, scarcely known, so that they appear to children as an alien and threatening cognitive style, though critical thinking in other modes may be familiar. For all these purposes the argument for curricular intervention is a powerful one, but the task is far from easy, and is prone to all the criticisms sometimes levelled at compensatory education on the grounds that one cognitive style should not be considered superior to another.

The remaining cognitive component is that of concepts. These fall into two groups. The first consists of the specific terms derived from the social disciplines: castle, peninsula, family, cost, tribe; the list could be prolonged almost indefinitely. Some of these facilitate general understanding, and it is likely that any lists of these that may be drawn up will show considerable overlap. Nevertheless, it is impossible to teach more than a limited number of them, even at the time of life when many children are prone to learn such concepts eagerly. The second kind of concept is more abstract and generalised, and can be considered in a hierarchy culminating in certain key concepts, of which *Place, Time and Society 8—13* identified four substantive examples: communication, power, values and beliefs, conflict/consensus; though this list might be amended by others. The choice of such concepts is itself problematic, but if they are borne in mind when actual subject matter is chosen and organised, then purpose is imparted to the curriculum process. Yet here again much depends on both development and experience. In some cultural situations, they are common currency; in others, scarcely comprehensible, and this is not simply a matter of active intelligence. It is therefore important to avoid a situation in which the principal concept learned is that the school cannot communicate its own intentions across the cultural gap.

In addition to the intellectual skills and concepts, there are social and physical skills, and attitudes and interests, to be considered. Social skills are a particular concern of this aspect of curriculum. They are a part of the approach to studying it, through group work and the skills of gaining information from adults by interviewing, as in family history studies (Steel and Taylor, 1973), and they are also a part of the general social education that is concerned with behaviour in groups and in society. At the same time, unlike what happens elsewhere in the curriculum, they are themselves part of what is studied. As the concept of a group becomes established, so the skills of group participation also develop, and the roles of groups within societies past and present come to be understood. Clearly, this too is dependent on the extent of group experience that children have undergone and are undergoing, and this gives rise to differences which again have to be countered by introducing into the curriculum an element of extension of experience. To do this in mathematics or art is valuable; to do it in place, time and society is essential.

Physical skills are less important, but they do play a part. Manipulative skills, such as the use of audio-visual apparatus, and expressive skills, such as the role of dance in enabling children to convey ideas by non-verbal means, are both examples of physical skills, and both may represent important differences in experience, while where physical defects are present, differences in development are clearly important too. However, this is part of the curriculum in general rather than being directly concerned with any one area.

Attitudes and interests, on the other hand, are very strongly related to place, time and society. Of the two terms, interests are probably the easier to discuss (Wilson, 1971). As with experience itself, they are frequently regarded as comprising both a subjective disposition and an object or objects of interest. Although it has sometimes been claimed that there is a general developmental trend in interests, it is heavily overlain by differences in experience, which is substantially linked with differences between families, localities, and other groups and subcultures. This clearly raises a question for curriculum, since if the children's culture limits interests, then an enabling curriculum will need to widen opportunities so that they can encounter more fields of knowledge and endeavour and thus meet with cultural growth. This involves value-judgements, since a mere extension of interests is not certain to ensure either growth in range or growth in what is desirable.

As for attitudes, it may seem inappropriate to refer to them here at all, since values and attitudes have been indicated as another facet of curriculum. This is true. Yet attitudes do also belong to place, time and society. Almost irrespective of the more fundamental attitudes that are central to children's self-concept, there are particular attitudes that betoken ways of looking at society. Prominent among these are two. One is caution about taking up any rigid point of view or adopting any rigid interpretation. With this goes a willingness to look to social-scientific procedures as a way of interpreting the world. A counterpart to this intellectual attitude is the willingness and readiness to exercise empathy. By empathy is here meant the cognitive and emotional capacity to identify with somebody else and to understand their position as it were from the inside, without adopting or supporting their point of view. Both of these attitudes are quite mature, and it may seem surprising that they should be regarded as within the scope of younger children at all. Much of the evidence, particularly about ethnic stereotypes among younger children, might appear to suggest that as with moral development, they are not yet ready for constructive scepticism or for the genuine exercise of empathy. Yet the experience of *Place, Time and Society 8-13* is that a sustained endeavour to develop these qualities in children at quite a young age is likely to bear fruit. Here again, of course, experience is a powerful factor, and it may well be that curricular intervention in this area is the most delicate and sensitive part of the approach to place, time and society: almost the most delicate part of the whole curriculum. Some studies of attitude change indicate, by their contradictory results, how problematic the task is, even when there is agreement in a school as to which attitudes are appropriate to foster. Where consensus on this point is markedly absent, then the curriculum may manifest reality, but at almost too high a price. What is more, it is necessary to steer carefully between a confident handing down of the teacher's (right) answer on the one hand, and a conveying on the other of an impression that because there is no one right answer, any old answer will do.

This consideration of skills, concepts, interests and attitudes as objectives indicates that there are many intricate issues to be borne in mind in designing a programme in place, time and society for younger children. However, there is one other consideration that must also be given due weight. It is one that would bulk much larger in a social-objectives model or an essentially forms-of-understanding model of curriculum, but cannot be swept aside in a process model either. It applies to this area of curriculum more, perhaps, than to any other. The point at issue is whether certain topics, certain questions, even certain aspects of content, have an unanswerable claim to be included irrespective of their contribution to the emergence of skills, concepts, attitudes and interests, because they represent a specific, prescribed extension of experience which every child ought to have. It is worth while to examine some of these.

One is the study of the local environment. There is no doubt that this is of great *illustrative* value in any curriculum. But there are also arguments for including it as a topic in its own right (Watts, 1969; Pluckrose, 1971). It can engender local loyalties and responsibilities. It can arouse a sense of the past and of tradition. It can bring to light local issues and problems, perhaps in a way that impels social criticism (Ward and Fyson, 1973). It can exemplify in an acute and immediate form the problems of environmental planning, pollution and control. In fact, this set of justifications for its inclusion sits easily alongside ways in which local study does subscribe to the general objectives of place, time and society, so tl a. in one sense the pursuit of those objectives is almost bound to point towards local study as a means of implementation. Nevertheless, these other reasons are advanced too, and any programme that embodies attention to the locality must take them into account.

A quite different kind of claim can be made on behalf of particular instances within time and place and, for different reasons, society. In the case of historical and geographical material, the claim is rather slender when it refers to particular events and places that all children ought to have heard about, if only because the selection of such a list must be arbitrary and must differ to a considerable extent from person to person. It is perhaps stronger when major elements of content are under review. The Roman Empire (though not its Chinese contemporary) and the geography of the homeland are examples of content which seem to have a strong claim and which often happen to be included in actual curricula, but even so, unless they can be justified on other grounds too, their claim may turn out to be more an embodiment of tradition than anything else. In any case there has to be heavy selection of content within such topics. Even so, the argument for familiarising children with the very broadest outlines of historical and geographical knowledge is not negligible, and even when the strict chronological and topographical appoach is eliminated, there is a good case for relating whatever content is chosen to the atlas of time as well as that of place. Much the same applies to some of the content of the social sciences. The family, for example, can be included specifically because families are so central to social organisation. If, however, there is an attempt to justify particular content on patriotic grounds, as part of a national heritage, whether it is the Tower of London or the Battle of Waterloo, or on particular political or religious grounds, that becomes a very different issue. For in that case the emphasis moves from the process curriculum towards the social-objectives pattern. Similarly, in an open democracy the values of open democracy itself and its institutions can claim inclusion on 'civic' grounds, as indeed they or their counterparts do in almost every other country. In many advanced societies today, again, stress is being laid on the need for adequate political, industrial and other economic education at the secondary level, and increasingly it is coming to be recognised that the foundations for such education can and should be laid at the primary level. This may involve a general historical, geographical or economic approach to local or other instances of industry, or perhaps a closer link with some particular industrial, agricultural or commercial venture. All of this is compatible with the general objectives of education in time, place and society, but it is the additional factor of a social imperative that is decisive in the actual choice of topic[4].

A somewhat similar claim for inclusion is that of preparation for living in a multi-ethnic society. There are of course many schools, especially in inner cities, where local studies can scarcely be introduced without also coming face to face with these wider issues on which much attention has recently been focused. But it is equally important that these issues shall also be deliberately introduced where they do not figure so conspicuously in the local environment. Since this raises questions both of knowledge and of attitudes, it refers to the value-attitude element in the curriculum as well as to place, time and society, but it is an example of a constraint that bears upon what particular instances of content may be chosen. It may be possible to develop particular skills, concepts and interests, and even attitudes of some sorts, without specific reference to this delicate matter, but there may be, in this one matter at least, a social imperative that cannot be set aside.

Once this has been accepted, of course, a similar claim can be made for every other socio-political issue, and then it becomes a matter of opinion and judgement where to draw the line between a process curriculum that is irresponsibly deficient in such content, and a social-imperatives curriculum that is dominated by it.

The distinction between a curriculum subordinated to social-imperatives claims and one that gives due place to the process approach is, in every case, a subtle one, but a very important one. It is virtually the difference between looking at development and experience in society as they are, and looking at them as, in somebody else's eyes, they ought to be. But even that is not clear enough. In a social-imperatives approach, they ought to be included because they are socially essential. If a process approach is to take adequate account of this claim, then it must itself make a considered response. The term 'responsible process approach' is perhaps appropriate within an enabling curriculum, one which is intended to widen horizons until there is sufficient basis in curricular experience to enable children to decide for themselves what ought to be.

Faced with all these considerations, as well as with the enormous extent of possible topics, it is not surprising that many teachers feel at a loss. They may even omit the interpretation of the social world because it is difficult for them, and console themselves by thinking that it is difficult for the children. For the task is a difficult one. There is no substitute for the process by which each school constructs its own approach, and this is necessary even in those national systems—the vast majority—in which curriculum is centrally prescribed. But if each school has to construct its own approach, it is also essential that this should be a purposive, structured approach.

There is no lack of valuable advice about syllabus-construction in general, considering objectives, organisation and content[5]. It is much less usual to find curricula in the social subjects directly related to development or experience. Both should be taken into account in planning any specific provision for the interpretation of the social world within an enabling curriculum.

At the age of 7, for example, children have rather a precarious hold on their mastery of reading and of written communication, and are still for the most part at a stage when systematic moral and social concerns are beyond them. Yet their experience has become varied and vivid, especially since television widened the visual world, and they can become deeply involved in projects on aspects of the local area, including individual and group work on drawing, painting or modelling of buildings, areas and people. From such activities they can build up their sense of place and their first attainments in graphicacy. As Boardman (1983) emphasises, there are specific skills which they can and should begin to acquire at that age. Meanwhile, they can also become engrossed in imaginative reconstruction of past or present, and in the beginnings of activities that are prominent in their own experience, such as communication (verbal and non-verbal) and writing. Indeed, this is a particularly clear instance of how a curriculum can intervene in the relation between development (increasing muscular co-ordination) and experience (perception of, and contact with, the world outside). To be sure, the 'product' of their individual and group work may appear rather spidery and may take a long time to materialise, but if it is linked with purposive talk and activity, then it serves a useful and constructive purpose. Seven is quite a difficult age to cater for in this part of the curriculum, but this challenge must be met through work based on the local area, on suitable themes from the past, and on social concepts related to their own lives as far as possible.

One year makes a considerable difference. At the age of 8 many children already have a reasonable mastery of reading and writing skills at a modest level, so that their capacity to undertake individual work now extends beyond non-book observation. Meanwhile, their social experience among themselves, and in society at large, becomes wider, and makes it possible to introduce more coherent social themes into the curriculum. Early societies, and simple parts of societies today, provide examples of topics that can be developed on a group basis and can thus also themselves help in social education. Some may choose to look at Stone Age communities, others at the Incas or the Norsemen, and still others at the surviving forest or desert-dwellers of today. In each case there is something of a dilemma, because such studies have to steer between patronising over-simplification on the one hand and stultifying detail and complexity on the other. They have also to avoid the danger that the study of simple societies might foster racial prejudices, especially since the children are not yet near the age at which black-and-white reasoning can be superseded.

Nevertheless, at the age of 9 they can reach a stage at which the spiral development of concepts and skills, as advocated by Bruner (1960) and others, has begun to take shape in a way which is applicable in schools generally, even if the actual content varies from class to class, school to school and year to year. The questions 'Where?' 'When?' 'Who?' 'How?' and 'Why?' introduced at the infant stage into the beginnings of interpreting the social world, should now have been taken considerably further.

From the age of 9 onwards, a marked expansion of themes can take effect. The diversity of actual topics chosen may in fact increase, but the common stock of skills and concepts can still be developed in parallel. Growing confidence in the exercise of physical and intellectual skills goes along with expansion and diversification of interests and a grasp of the need for specialised knowledge. Quite ambitious studies of the local area become possible, alongside instances from past and present societies which emphasise such features as the probabilistic thinking mentioned earlier (there is no one right answer, but some more likely than others), the scrutiny of evidence of all kinds, and the discussion of moral and ethical themes. There is no stage of primary education at which the combination of motivation with capacity is more marked than between 9 and 12, and it is no exaggeration to claim that the foundations of citizenship can be laid at this time. This implies both understanding, in more than one of the forms, and critical awareness which is compatible with social imperatives of a democratic nature. One particularly valuable use of experience at this stage is to start from where the children are, and to extend outwards by means of a journey, or a story, or a family tree, or whatever structured device opens the doors of place, time and society so that the conventional representation of place (by map and atlas) and time (by time-line and its associated vocabulary) is brought naturally into use. This constitutes in fact a further twist of the spiral curriculum, one within which knowledge of one theme, that of the locality, becomes more substantial. Within this local area it is now possible to practise the skills of history (finding and interpreting evidence), or geography (observing and mapping), of economics (value and trade), or sociology and politics (decision-making and value considerations) and even of social psychology, as the children come to consider what the locality means to them individually and collectively, and which parts they know, like, or fear most. Yet by alternating local studies with those remote in place and time and concerning very different societies, they can avoid the snares of parochialism.

It is one stage beyond this to prescribe an actual curriculum in the interpretation of the social world. There are many instances of such curricula[6]. The important point to emphasise in the present discussion is that, by interaction with development and experience, the questions 'Where?' 'When?' 'Who?' 'How?' and 'Why?' can be carried from the infant years through to a point at which they reach a disciplined introduction to the interpretation of the social world in later years.

Of course, work of this kind need not take place continuously, every day or week throughout primary education. It may be done in bursts, with perhaps science taking over in the intervening periods. What does matter is that over the whole span of primary education it should be fairly represented in a structured progression.

It is then necessary for any school to undertake the actual planning of this element in an enabling curriculum, in the light of all the relevant circumstances. First, it requires the establishment of a measure of agreement among the staff of the school, not only about the purpose of an enabling curriculum, but also about the means by which it can be brought into being, the innovation that is required. The next step is less certain, for it can take either of two forms.

The first of these is by firming up the programme for just one class, with a teacher selecting what appears suitable and then planning, say, two major themes, to be included somewhere in the programme for that class during a year in school. Each theme should then be suitable for that stage in the development of the particular class, in terms of its collective development and experience. The two should embody balance (it must not all be about the same kind of social content) and also structure and progression (it should never be random and repetitive, but should in some way figure in a sequence).

Often it is impossible to start an innovation of this kind in any way except through the solo effort of one teacher. But already it will be clear that the whole process can be greatly assisted if a school embarks on the venture as a unit. For then the process of planning for sequential growth over the years is greatly facilitated. At first this is likely to be viewed with some scepticism, as an interference with the autonomy of teachers and with that version of the process curriculum that regards spontaneity as a paramount virtue. However, an *enabling* curriculum must, by definition, involve intervention and not just response. A broad framework of themes leaves sufficient scope for adaptation to current experience to make possible the immediacy and relevance that are needed, while bearing the longer-term goals in mind. As has already been emphasised, the essential point of policy must be to emphasise the process elements such as skill and concept formation, rather than content areas, in each year, and to determine how these process elements relate to those in the other parts of the curriculum: science, and the five

## The Interpretation of the Social World 97

others considered in Chapter 5. Once this sequence is agreed as a realistic one for the school concerned, it becomes possible to spell out broad areas of content. For the choice of these, the inclinations of teachers and the availability of instances are among the influences that should, legitimately, be considered.

The next step is, as before, to launch at least one actual scheme of work. All eyes will then be on this one, to see how it develops and to learn from it. For it then becomes a part of the professional development and experience of the teachers themselves. Within the normal pattern of English primary education it is unlikely that a distinctive set of schemes for the interpretation of the social world will be introduced below the age of 7, though social considerations may well figure in the programme for infants. However, there is something to be said for making the first venture with the first year in the junior school, or the first year in a middle school, so that the innovation can be extended upwards. In other systems too, the age of 8 would be a good starting-point, with 9 as a possible alternative. The greater maturity and initiative of children at the upper end of the school sometimes tempts teachers to start with them, but this has the disadvantage that they are, as it were, phased out of primary education almost at once. It also has the further disadvantage that the separateness of the elements in the curriculum is more definite then, so that the cross-curricular value of an innovation in place, time and society is more difficult to achieve. But at the age of 7 to 8 an innovation is likely to be seen in perspective. For example, it may figure only in one term out of the three, or in parts of two terms, receiving quite intense consideration while it is in force and then giving place to something emphasising one of the other elements, which is all to the good, provided that the overall balance is preserved and the aims of enablement remembered.

Similar suggestions can be made about the rest of the curriculum, but each really requires a depth of familiarity with that particular aspect. So the process of building an enabling curriculum is not a trivial one. Yet this is only a part of the school's programme, and the school's programme is only part of the experience of children that interacts with their development. In the next three chapters some of the wider aspects and implications of an enabling curriculum are considered.

## Notes

1. I had the privilege of directing the Schools Council project *History, Geography and Social Science 8–13* during its first three years 1971–4. The more manageable title *Place, Time and Society 8–13* was soon adopted and continues to be used. I am indebted to my colleagues in the project team—Ray Derricott, Keith Cooper, Gordon Elliott, Hazel Sumner, and Allan Waplington—for many of the ideas embodied in this chapter and elsewhere. The main publication from the project is Blyth, W.A.L. *et al. Place, Time and Society 8–13: Curriculum Development in History, Geography and Social Science* (Collins/ESL Bristol, 1976) now available from ES Training Services Ltd, Waverley Road, Yate, Bristol BS17 5RB.

2. The Environmental Studies Project was directed by Melville T. Harris and worked substantially in Wales, particularly on historical and geographical aspects of environment. Its publications are handled by Rupert Hart-Davis.

3. For an exploration of the potentialities of historical material with young children, see Blyth, J.E. (1982) *History in Primary Schools*, McGraw Hill.

4. While engaged in the preparation of this book, I have been co-operating with a working party under the aegis of the Schools Council Industry Project, considering the possibilities of developing Industry Education with younger children. It is hoped that a publication will follow with a title such as *Primary School and the Working World*. See also 5, p. 151 below.

5. Two of the most useful books, apart from those already mentioned, are: Mills, D. (ed.), (1981) *Geographical Work in Primary and Middle Schools*, Geographical Association; and for a more comprehensive view of syllabus-construction in the social subjects as a whole, Lawton, D. *et al.* (1971)

6. Among the most useful sources for examples of actual curricula are local education authorities. In some cases, groups of teachers, working with advisors, have formulated 'agreed syllabuses' in the interpretation of the social world which command broadly based assent in their own areas and are valuable as starting-points for thinking elsewhere.

# 7 DEVELOPMENT, EXPERIENCE AND THE WIDER CURRICULUM

Nowadays it is almost a truism that the informal part of the curriculum, its organisational aspect and also the hidden curriculum have to be considered alongside their formal counterpart. In Chapter 3 their importance was mentioned briefly; here they will be introduced in more detail.

The informal curriculum will be taken to mean all the planned and intended part of a school's programme that lies outside the formal curriculum itself. It is true that if there is a range of these 'extra-curricular' activities, they are part of the hidden curriculum in the sense that they express the school's value-system, both through what is included and through what is excluded. Thus, not every school has a chess club or a recorder group, or an annual school journey for the 9-year-olds, or whatever it may be. However, the activities themselves are not hidden: on the contrary, it is likely that they will be drawn assiduously to the attention of staff, parents, pupils, governors, and perhaps particularly to those who exercise authority, outside the school. The organisational curriculum, or 'institutional curriculum', to use Joan Dean's term (1983), extends beyond these activities. The school rules obviously embody values. So, less obviously, does the way in which the school's public places are used. If the corridors are replete with pottery, that conveys one kind of value. If there is an honours board, showing who has gained entry to what secondary school over the years, that conveys another. So does the style of control that is maintained. Beyond this again lies the hidden curriculum: the *mores* implemented by the head and the staff, and the values that they approve, or disapprove, however subtly, and the extent to which these values are held in common or become the subject of dispute. These values may be related to particular issues, such as the relative importance of creativity and of introduction to a heritage of literature or art or music. They may be related too to particular social groups and their values, whether this concerns social class or religious or ethnic groups, in which case the whole problem of stereotypes is raised. Or they may apply specifically to patterns of behaviour that are considered appropriate or inappropriate for children according to their age and sex. Taken together, all of these values combine into what is sometimes termed the ethos of the school, a subject which is more likely to invite comment than to succumb to easy analysis.

If an enabling curriculum consists of intervention in the interaction of development with experience, this will also be true of the informal, organisational and hidden curricula. In fact it is likely to be more true of them.

One reason for this is that they cannot be easily rendered into subjects, or considered mainly in terms of content. So much of what they include is in practice related to what is deemed appropriate to start at a particular age-level and then continue in a developmental sequence. Starting the violin or safety training on bicycles is often seen and planned as something for a particular age-level, say, 8. The choice of individuals to undertake such activities is, however, often made in terms of experience. Meanwhile, just because there is a collective impression of what should be the ethos for children of a particular age-level, this can be conveyed through the rules and assumptions that pervade each class as well as the school as a whole. There is in such circumstances no need to call for a spiral curriculum: this part of the curriculum is already conceived in terms of spiral development of values and monitored by graded testing. Here too the very fact that values are conveyed obliquely means that their relation to previous experience and the resultant readiness to accept and absorb values is particularly important. There is little overt, collective teaching to act as a common input. Yet in this sensitive part of the school's programme, where its impact is particularly important, the actual relation of the informal and hidden curriculum to development and experience is not usually worked out in detail. This issue will now be examined more extensively, in relation to the different parts of the informal and organisational curriculum, and then of the hidden curriculum, and finally these will be considered in relation to the six aspects of the formal curriculum itself.

The *informal curriculum*, that is to say those official activities that are arranged outside school time, is a feature of the upper rather than the lower primary years. This is partly because the individual activities do largely depend on a general level of hand-eye coordination and fine muscular control, and also of personal independence, that is not usual before the age of 7 or 8. This is true of many physical activities. Some of these, such as swimming, begin within the formal curriculum and then generate individual activities beyond it. Much the same is in fact true of games and competitive sports, especially for boys.

Indeed, boys' games are in themselves a very interesting and important topic. They may take the form of a two-tier strategy. A whole year-group may be taken out to the field to play what is preponderantly in most countries, football. This may begin as one, two, or two-and-a-bit, games, within which some form of talent-spotting soon begins. From this a representative team gradually emerges. Some members are very keen and quite capable, and may then receive further direct coaching as part of the informal curriculum. If there is a teacher adept in coaching and very keen on developing competitive football with other schools, he may invade the formal curriculum with an extension of the informal, at the expense of the rest of the pupils. If he does, and if (as sometimes happens) he is allowed a priority in use of the school telephone that others do not have, then this conveys a message not only in the informal but also in the hidden curriculum. It implies that in this, or in any school worth its salt, that is the status that competitive football ought to occupy. More rarely, the same can apply to other games, including girls' games, and to athletics or swimming. But football is usually the prime claimant.

Its relation to experience is more intriguing. Individual boys may develop the skills of football partly because of their physique. They are much more likely to do so because of their experience of playing football before they even come to school, and of continuing to do so outside school. Some may flourish also in other competitive football such as Saturday or Sunday leagues, which may eventually challenge the school itself for their allegiance. In any case much depends on the particular circumstances in which individual children find themselves. Some have a flying start in the popular game. Others, for example for family reasons, receive such an early and intensive introduction to other games that they identify themselves from an early age with, for example, tennis.

Other informal activities depend more on intellectual development. An obvious example is chess. It can scarcely be learned in the earlier primary years, owing to the patterns of reasoning which require a suitable level of maturation, yet once this is attained, some individuals can progress with extraordinary rapidity. Sometimes this is due to a home environment in which chess figures prominently, or to a close friendship with an established chess player, but in this case the school does seem able to generate a particular pattern of interest that can in its turn spill over into other fields of experience. Something similar applies to the playing of musical instruments, where there is a fairly regular pattern of habituation, with the simpler, lighter, more fashionable and less costly instruments coming usually first, and being taken up by a sizeable minority of children, although there are rarer instances of others in the primary years. This kind of activity has a clear relation to growing physical skills, but experience can play quite a decisive part in predisposing children to an interest in instrumental music. This experience may be through an organisation such as the Salvation Army, but it is far more likely to be derived from membership of a musical family. Sometimes, of course, children associate with others who do belong to musical families. However, there are certainly some for whom the interest in instrumental music stems from the school itself, and it may be difficult for a school to ensure that a majority interest in the guitar does not crowd out the minority who would take to the violin or the oboe.

Other aspects of the informal curriculum depend more closely on social/emotional development. They include short class expeditions, to some extent linked with the formal curriculum, and also informal social occasions either within the school, or shared with the adult community. Here too the importance of experience is evident, since there is a considerable advantage for those already accustomed to activities of this kind. However, there is an excellent opportunity for a school to intervene decisively and to support those to whom the activity is novel, and those who display unsuspected talents when free from the constraints of the formal curriculum itself. Social/emotional development is also relevant to activities of other kinds such as choirs and orchestras and displays of dance drama, since they require a certain level of social maturity in order to ensure co-operation, while the sense of drama that surrounds the actual performance is itself an important element, one which can also exercise quite an influence on the staff.

In addition to the significance of its various parts, the informal curriculum as a whole signals a message. If there is, as it were, too much of it, then everybody's contribution may tend to become reluctant and perfunctory. Of course, it is not easy to find time, space or teachers to run such activities, least of all at a time when economies are being made in every direction, as they are to a greater or lesser extent in so many countries. There can then be an opportunity for the informal curriculum to signal another message, that of welcome to the surrounding community. For this is one way in which parents and other adults can volunteer to alleviate shortages. There is perhaps a special place here for adults who might otherwise feel unwanted, including those unemployed or prematurely retired as well as those beyond the normal retiring age. It is, of course, necessary in such cases to obtain the approval of the teachers' unions, but in activities of this kind there is scarcely any competition with what teachers do, or threat to their jobs.

On the other hand, if there is too little of the informal curriculum in a school there develops a void into which out-of-school experience can spill over. Moreover, this too carries messages for the community, such as that teachers do not or will not take a broad interest in children's educational progress, and that the social relationships familiar in the streets and fields can be unblushingly continued and modified in the playground or the nearby croft because there is nothing better to do in school. Sometimes this state of affairs is simply unavoidable if teachers are to have any break in their duties, but the consequences too are inescapable. A school which limits its impact on experience in terms of time will be liable also to limit its impact in terms of influence.

No discussion of the informal curriculum is complete without some reference to the many informal agencies of education that operate outside the school: youth organisations, Sunday schools, football leagues and youth choirs, bands and orchestras, to mention only a few. In some schools they almost form a part of the curriculum itself; this is specially true of boarding schools. In many others the informal curriculum is designed in such a way as to permit these informal agencies outside school to complement the school curriculum in a relatively planned fashion. That is only possible where there is a high degree of concordance between the two, as may be the case in village schools and also in some denominational schools. It is informative to remember that it is in the Soviet Union that this concordance is most complete, so much so that matters normally considered as a part of the curriculum in the West are systematically assigned to the Octobrists or the Young Pioneers. But in many situations in Western countries it is impossible to do more than to ensure that schools take note of this alternative source of experience, and bring it too into the interaction with development for which an enabling curriculum must plan. Incidentally, it is also incumbent on the various organisations to design their own programmes as a form of intervention in the relation of experience with development.

The *organisational* curriculum consists of the rules that the school observes and the way in which authority and control are exercised. Since, according to the studies of Piaget and Kohlberg and their followers which were mentioned in Chapter 5, children at the primary level are in transition from a stage of rule-governed behaviour to one in which rules are at least partially questioned, the importance of rules in relation to development is evident. Where there is institutional separation between the youngest children and the rest, as between infants and juniors, or between first and middle schools in England, it becomes possible to cater partially for this developmental difference by having different sets of rules for the two schools. Even so, there is a considerable span of social development within the junior or middle school, and more so in a six-year span such as is found in primary schools in many other countries. There is nothing illogical or undesirable about this. In fact, a case can be made out for maintaining a set of rules which children first learn to accept and then learn to scrutinise. Much the same, of course, takes place in secondary schools. Eventually, it even becomes possible for the children to help to determine some of the rules, as part of their political and social education.

What is important is that the rules should be, as far as possible, matched with the social development of the children, so that there is a case for having rules for each class in addition to rules for the school. To pitch these rules correctly involves a compromise between the tendency for the children, especially the younger ones, to evolve complicated rituals of rule-making (Sluckin, 1981) and the need for the rules to be few, simple and unambiguous, with straightforward justifications. Anybody can see why there should be no running in the corridors, even when they want to run there.

The relationship between rules and experience is more complex. At the specific level, children may encounter expectations and even commands in school which are entirely different from those they meet elsewhere. Differences in social-class expectations have for some time been widely recognised as important here, but more recently it has been seen that still greater differences may apply in the case of ethnic minorities. Instances are regularly cited of differences in clothing, in feeding, or in aspects of behaviour in which minorities such as Sikhs find themselves acutely at variance with school procedures. There is no easy solution to this issue.

One approach is to have a pluralist code, whereby children in each group conform to its own practices. There is much to be said for this, though difficulties are bound to arise at the margins of groups where individuals may not be sure to which of two they should give their principal allegiance. Difficulties may also arise when one group suspects that another is being treated more indulgently.

Irrespective of groups of cultural differences, there are others relating to family situations. An eldest child in the younger primary years may be habitually regarded at home as one who helps to enforce the rules, while at school their age-level is such that they are assumed to require rules to be enforced upon them. The exact converse applies to a youngest child in the older primary years. Only children may find it difficult to adjust from the home in which rules are made for a child (with or without his or her assistance) to the school in which rules are made by, or imposed on, children together. So the perceptions of rules are rendered by experience essentially unequal, embedded in distributive justice. All children who become a genuine part of a school community also have in any case to come to terms with the differences between the rules that are evolved within their peer groups and the rules developed by the school to govern formal relationships within the curriculum and organisation of the school. In these respects a primary school is not only a microcosm of society, but an essential introduction to society.

All of this assumes at least a modicum of agreement that rules, as such, are needed. The problem becomes more difficult when groups are encountered that do not have such rules, or whose rules are deliberately devised for a different purpose. In Islam, in Judaism, in Catholic or Protestant Christianity, the function of rules is seen as differently embedded in the social process. This does not apply simply to particular rules, but to the notion of rule-governed behaviour itself. Therefore, it does not just apply to religious customs or precepts, but to any other kind of rule-making including rules in school. If keeping the rules rigidly is regarded as essential, that is a very different matter from regarding the rules as at best a guide to what depends on the Holy Spirit. Even if the latter allows a place for a civil code in a secular society, that becomes a concession to human frailty rather than the basis for human conduct. Experience in an adult community which holds the one view or the other can result in very different basic responses to school rules, even when filtered through the processes of intellectual and social development among children. Beyond this again there are the puzzlements aroused in those from unusual communities in which explicit rules have virtually no place, as with some Quakers and even some drop-out communes. In all of these cases a school conveys, simply by dint of having rules, the hidden message that one ought to have rules, that anybody who doesn't is both wrong and anti-social, and that however the school's rules happen to have been compiled, those are the rules that must be obeyed, and the people who drew them up have the right to do so. According to the followers of Piaget and Kohlberg, that is what most primary children, at heart, believe.

Further social education is embodied in the authority-structure of the school itself. During the primary years children's social development reaches a point at which, as was suggested in Chapter 6, the working of a social organisation becomes comprehensible to them. As they grow a little older, and before they leave the primary school, they are able to see further into the relation between social institutions and others. Inevitably, as Durkheim, Dewey and Parsons[1] all realised, the school itself, together with its component classes, is the social unit which is most open to them to understand as individuals, and also most available for them to study as a collectivity. Just as parents and siblings, neighbours and peers, had previously enacted the prototypes of adult roles, so now this function comes to be assumed by teachers. At first this applies mainly within one class: that is the case below the age of 7 or 8. At that stage the one-to-one relationship between teacher and class merits strong support. Later, as the relation of class to class and teacher to teacher becomes more evident, more co-operation and exchange between classes and teachers becomes desirable.

Previous experience is relevant to both poles of this process. Intense experience within a family unit, or its total absence, both spell problems for the establishment of relations with a teacher. Later, when the social horizon widens, there is an advantage for those children who are already accustomed to moving in wider social groups, and also for those whose wider social groups correspond most closely to the teachers' own. So here too there is a built-in inequality based on prior and concurrent experience.

At the upper end of a primary school children become aware, to some extent, of adult relationships, and at the upper end of the primary school may themselves acquire quasi-adult roles (Blyth, 1965) which conceal the real gulf in maturity between their teachers and themselves. As they become aware of the different adults and their relationships, questions of hierarchy and authority become apparent and may lead children momentarily to combine with, or against, a teacher, absorbing meanwhile general ideas of how these matters are handled by adults. It seems probable that perceived differences in the administrative climates of primary schools themselves affect the impressions children form of adult relationships, formal and informal, and it would be fascinating to examine the outcome of a study as thorough as Paisey's (1981), but devoted to children's, rather than teachers' responses. Some, but not much, can be found in the general literature on the social psychology of schools.

Grouping is another significant feature of the organisational curriculum. For it affects children's learning and behaviour and at the same time conveys messages about how groups do, and should behave. They learn in school, as in families, how to relate to other children of their own and other ages, and sex, temperament and ability.

Ability grouping, in the form of streaming, has been the most important kind of grouping in primary schools in recent years (Barker Lunn, 1970). In the past twenty years it has decreased considerably, though some forms of within-class ability grouping remain and may even be increasing. The extent of ability grouping in itself proclaims one set of values held by a school.

Grouping by temperament, or rather by friendship, is an approach that has often been advocated, though it may turn out to be a disguised form of ability grouping or a means of fomenting disruptive behaviour, and may thus be deliberately countered by official policy in some schools. This kind of grouping does at least indicate that the school is concerned about social as well as cognitive affairs, but the nature of its implementation points out the nature of that concern.

Especially among older juniors, friendship and other informal groups tend to be single-sex in character. It is as though each sex draws apart from the other (Blyth, 1965, Ch. 3) as part of its social development (heavily reinforced by experience) through which it attains a collective identity. This process can be accentuated and stereotyped, or alternatively modified and combated, through curricular experience and through the ways in which children are officially grouped both inside and outside the classroom. In any school it is significant to note what policy is adopted on this issue, and also how far girls are thereby habitually encouraged to be relatively demure, sensitive and limited in their responses, activities and aspirations, while boys are urged to be more physically vigorous, tough, jolly and enterprising. Attention has been increasingly drawn to such processes (e.g. Clarricoats, 1980). They are not universal, but they are yet another feature of the organisational curriculum which can be very influential. A class in which it is a punishment for a boy to be told to sit among the girls is one that spells out several social lessons through that very situation.

A further aspect of grouping is that of mixed-age combinations. When children of different ages are taught together, this enables them to see themselves clearly on a developmental ladder, and they are often avid for the next stage, the one that they have firmly fixed in their sights. One way in which they can reinforce their present status and build on it is by helping in turn those younger than themselves. The nineteenth-century monitorial system did have a positive feature here, though it was far too cheap and mechanical in practice to be commended now. In the USA the term 'cascade teaching' is used to denote this process, and the comprehensive study of children as teachers by Allen (1976) conveys some idea of what can be achieved, and when. In England vertical grouping and family grouping have been advocated and practised partly because they allow of just this kind of procedure, together with other social advantages such as stability (Ridgway and Lawton, 1968), but also partly on account of the small size of some schools, which leaves little option, or the need to respond to open-plan assumptions (Bennett *et al.*, 1980). Bruner has commented interestingly on the value of the 'intermediate generation' between teachers and young children as transmitters of ideas, capable of rendering adult conceptions into patterns of language and thought more akin to those of the youngest. This has something in common, at the individual level, with the collective practice of *shevstvo* in Soviet schools (Bronfenbrenner, 1970) whereby one class virtually adopts a younger one. This form of grouping is of particular interest because it necessarily takes development into account in its very processes, and is also parallel to much informal experience in homes and neighbourhoods.

In all of these ways it is clear that the actual children with whom any particular child interacts are very influential for subsequent development and experience, and can make or mar for the individual whatever sets of learning experiences are designed for him or her. The possibilities of constructive interaction are greater where

## Development, Experience and the Wider Curriculum 109

children have more combinations with which to experiment, and fewer unhappy situations within which they are trapped. Thus, in an enabling curriculum there is a strong argument for providing all children with a progressively greater range of group experiences as they grow older. These may extend from whole-class participation, as in infant story and music, through various kinds of group work in language and number with different combinations of children and the exploration of the social and physical world, to teams for games and essentially individual activities as in art, craft and some aspects of PE. Such variety can combat stereotypes of age, sex, temperament or ability, and can encourage every individual to construct a positive and diverse self-image, along with the 'self-curriculum' referred to in Chapter 5. If this appears to smack of social engineering, this is only because it might develop into social engineering in a social-imperatives framework. Where a process approach predominates, as an enabling curriculum requires, then the outcome of a policy of diversity in grouping should be an increase in the enrichment and diversification of curricular and general experience in school and perhaps beyond. Certainly, this aspect of the organisational curriculum is of central importance in the design of an enabling curriculum, and a sensitive grouping policy indicates to children that a school is concerned to emphasise the importance of learning to learn and live together.

The *hidden curriculum* consists of those values and attitudes which are conveyed through incidental comments or even through gestures and other non-verbal means. The scope for speculation about such matters is enormous, and they figure substantially also in the general literature on school curriculum, organisation and ethos[2]. In many ways the hidden curriculum is a challenge to teachers to avoid either of two extremes, both of which appear ridiculous when spelled out, but both of which in their subtler forms can be pervasive. The first of these is the projection on to children of aspects of behaviour that are admired in adults. The other is the attempt to keep children as Peter Pans, young, amusing and innocent. Cutting across these possibilities is another dimension with two extremes of which one is unisex and the other exaggerates the masculinity of boys and the femininity of girls. These may be termed respectively the adult/baby dimension and the sex/unisex dimension. A third important feature is the stereotype/individual dimension. By this is meant the tendency to group children together in thinking about them, or to avoid doing so. At its extremes this too has a smack of absurdity in it, but it is very pervasive. In an enabling curriculum it is obviously desirable to lean towards the individual end of this dimension, but it is not always done. Every teacher has, consciously or unconsciously, some combination of attitudes on these dimensions and when the teachers in a school, set in their respective places in the power structure, express these attitudes together, either in conflict or in consensus, the outcome is the hidden curriculum itself.

The relation of the hidden curriculum to development and experience is a matter of considerable importance. Initially, because children at the beginning of school life are relatively small and dependent, their limited development often evokes a response in which the 'baby' and 'unisex' poles of these distributions are emphasised, though the 'individual' emphasis is also marked. As the children grow older, these emphases change, differently for different teachers and in different situations. Children too react differently, and so the hidden curriculum makes its differential impact.

Within this developmental pattern, critical incidents may take place which determine changes in the hidden agenda. In this way the effect of experience is felt. Ethnographic studies of individual classes have indicated how this takes place[3], and the hidden curriculum embodies the ways in which teachers react, individually and collectively, to incidents among children. That reaction is in turn affected by the extent to which the stereotype pole comes to predominate in the third distribution, and in particular, how major groups in society are viewed.

Assumptions about groups are part of the stock-in-trade of any serious educational discussion. The most dramatic kind is concerned with ethnic differences which are themselves often (but not always) conspicuous, but which give rise to subtle and little-noticed responses. Even when stereotypes are consciously combated, they may still be influential and reinforced in unexpected ways. One teacher may think of Wayne as a remarkably poised, thoughtful and co-operative West Indian boy; another teacher may not think of him as a West Indian at all, but just as another individual. There is a distinct difference between the two in respect of the hidden curriculum. Similar considerations apply to social-class or rural/urban differences and, still more pervasively, to sex-differences. The ways in which teachers talk to, and about, children, can probably convey far more than is intended, especially in view of the attitudes and friendship patterns that frequently exist (Davey and Mullin, 1982).

The same consideration can apply also to families. A new arrival with the same features, the same non-verbal traits, even the same kind of clothing as a notorious elder sibling can cause a teacher to bristle and stiffen slightly even while welcoming him or her. Even if this inherited mantle does not fall on an individual, an early reputation becomes difficult to slough off and can be intensified if one teacher, talking to another and apparently out of earshot, makes a comment and looks meaningfully in the child's direction. Of course, it is difficult for a teacher to catch himself or herself in the act of conveying such information, especially since there is a strong case for showing some kinds of compensatory and even preferential treatment to children whose home or peer relations leave them disadvantaged. Like so much else in primary teaching, this is a matter for fine judgement.

Mention of peer relations raises another aspect of the hidden curriculum of a primary school, one that is particularly difficult to examine because of the cross-currents of values that it exposes. In a purely mechanical model of children's behaviour, an enabling curriculum, effectively implemented, should eliminate impediments to social harmony. The balance of evidence may well be in favour of a positive relationship between that curriculum and a reduction in social tension. But that is a very different matter from eliminating it. Developmental considerations alone indicate that social tensions in a school are likely to persist while children remain at the stage of moral growth normal at their age. Principled reasons for deviance from normal behaviour involve something literally beyond them, part of the strange adult world, and the passionate enforcement of what appears fair punishment is more typical. A newcomer is viewed with suspicion unless he or she brings an obvious asset such as skill in ball games, a sense of fun and humour, and good looks. Even then, an elementary test of acceptability is often set. For others the test is harder. Failure, or partial success, may be followed by an agonised period of exclusion from social groups at an age when membership matters very acutely, or even by sustained verbal or physical aggression. Often the perpetuation of such distress arises from an inability to master the repertoire of accepted codes of response, as Sluckin (1981) has demonstrated, which in its turn results from previous experience that is little use, or even positively disadvantageous, for social adjustment. For example, a boy from a small country school where girls were in a majority and girls' games predominated is likely to have a difficult time if translated to a large boys' school, or even a large mixed school, in a city. For the few concerned this can be a decisive interaction between development and experience.

The hidden curriculum of the school is then shown by the way in which the staff respond. In the first place it is even indicated by whether they notice. If they notice, then it is shown by whether they embark on an over-protective intervention, or whether they dismiss an incident as trivial or as boys being boys, or as girls being harmless because they do not employ sticks and stones to break bones. In most cases, no doubt, a school claims to strike a suitable balance between these extremes. This claim may be exaggerated. It is easy to forget that school experience is unequal in its impact; that some incidents constitute drama and are remembered (witness the audience that soon gathers round a 'real' fight); that for the disadvantaged individuals, and some others, this kind of experience can be disproportionate and even decisive in determining response to school; and that to everyone, a message is conveyed about the boundary that does and ought to exist between the official domain and space of a school—and hence of other social institutions—and the private spaces that lie outside its cognisance.

Many more instances of the hidden curriculum could be given, with indications of its interrelation with development and experience. Clearly, if there is to be an enabling curriculum, encouraging choice and acceptance among all the children, it must have consequences for the hidden as well as the informal and organisational curriculum. Yet this can be achieved only if there is, first, a genuine realisation of the ways in which the wider curriculum operates, and in any school this may require a process of collective acquisition of awareness. It may be of some relevance to this self-awareness to consider the relation of the wider curriculum to the six aspects of the formal curriculum discussed in Chapter 5, against the backgrounds of development and experience in children.

The impact of the wider curriculum on growth, health and movement has already been mentioned. Simply because of their palpable visibility and of the delight that children take in their developing powers, particular attention is paid to the ways in which this topic figures in the informal and hidden programme. If a school indicates through its value-system that prowess in football or swimming is disproportionately valued, then this message is likely to register. So is the accompanying message, readily conveyed, that the individuals who shine at the favoured activities are somehow personally more important. Oddly, this message may be almost deliberately conveyed in order to counteract the alternative message that academic prowess is what matters. It may be done in the name of equality; it may result merely in the substitution of one kind of inequality for another, not necessarily more defensible. More important is the way in which the hidden curriculum affects sex education. A sensitive awareness of the changes overtaking children, and of the substitute lore that they absorb, rather than a rather precious attempt to preserve innocence, conveys the realisation that the school itself is aware. Smoking, which is in some primary schools widespread, has to be considered in a broader sense than in a project on the human body, but again in an informative sense rather than as prohibition, in the full realisation that some children will become smokers, just as some teachers are.

The question of smoking illustrates rather clearly where teachers stand on each of the three dimensions: adult/baby; sex/unisex; stereotype/individual. There is also significance in the setting in which pronouncements are made about such matters. If they are announced to a whole-school assembly, that may attach some awe to the message at the expense of personal emphasis: a one-to-one meeting in a headteacher's room could have the opposite significance. Needless to say, a teacher who declaims against children smoking, and himself or herself smokes, conveys yet another message. Whatever the message, it is likely to be powerful if it refers to growth, health and movement.

The wider curriculum is at least equally important in learning about communication. For the school is a communication system. There is evidently a use of language systems for everyday messages, spoken or written. This not only embodies, but encourages, use of language for this purpose, and this at least is usually uncomplicated. When there is a bilingual problem and Welsh, or Creole, or Urdu is usually spoken in everyday experience, then the outcome is less straightforward. For although the official communications may help in the learning of English, or its counterpart as official language, the life of the school may itself convey the impression that there is something inferior, as well as unusual, about other languages. Non-verbal languages are still more prominent in the wider curriculum, since facial and other gestures are the very embodiment of much of the hidden curriculum. Not only do they confirm (or modify) a child's self-concept, they also reinforce the impression that this is the way in which such messages are conveyed. Some children are more alert than others to the messages themselves, and they for their part gain doubly, by learning what the non-verbal language is, and by learning that facility in its use is an advantage. In comparison with these uses of formal and non-verbal communication systems, the wider curriculum does not involve much use of number systems as communication, which remains *par excellence* the business of the formal curriculum itself, as it has been for so long. Only recently has this come to be slightly modified by the introduction of computers which, through the general extent to which they are used as well as their possibilities in a computer club or other informal activity, or encouraged as a home pursuit, can proclaim the importance attaching to such matters.

The importance of scientific understanding of the world of nature can be stressed by what is chosen to display in an entrance hall, and it can be very genuinely and effectively concentrated on what appear to be unpromising subjects, such as the sheep's eye that crowned a particular study in a school I knew. Its centrality conveyed that 'science' was not something confined to a classroom or an interest table but deserved to be more widely shown. However, the wider curriculum can, and does inevitably, do more to exemplify understanding of the social world. For just as the school is a communication system, so it is also inevitably a social organisation. Here too the display of illustrations of other times and lands can convey what is regarded as important enough to figure in a public space. Much more importantly, it exemplifies essential features of social organisation: hierarchy, consensus, conflict, sex-roles, mechanisms of social control, and the regulative functions of myth and ritual, to mention only some. One very obvious and important feature, which the children themselves are well aware of, is the relationship between work and social relationships. Indeed, teachers often use children's social relationships as a means of stimulating work (Bossert, 1979; Galton, Simon and Croll, 1980). Another social feature, also evident to children, is that of teaching style (Bennett, 1976; Galton *et al.*, 1980). If the school itself is then legitimated as a proper subject for consideration in the formal curriculum, then that formal curriculum becomes less isolated and more meaningful. At the same time there is the opposite risk that by subjecting, however slightly, its own system of communication and control to scrutiny by those who are to be controlled, its control will be eroded. This is a very genuine issue, which permits of no simple

## Development, Experience and the Wider Curriculum 115

answer when development is taken into account, but which remains critical in relation to experience. It is one way in which the social environment is, and has to be, both part of the context of primary education and part of its content.

The wider curriculum is a very important means of developing vision and imagination. Schools have not been slow to seek to present Whitehead's (1932) 'habitual vision of greatness'. Religious schools are constrained to place the Cross, or the Star of David, or whichever symbol is most important to their own faith, in the centre of things. In many countries the national flag calls constantly for recognition. Readings from the Bible, the Koran, or the collective study of Marxism-Leninism all embody some element of vision as well as of belief. Even when there is a deliberate absence of such commitment, children may be accustomed to trooping into their assembly past a Rembrandt or a Turner or a Picasso, to the strains of Mozart on the record-player, before hearing a simple tale or poem from a 'good' modern author. Such proceedings may provoke ridicule or hostility from those who would rather see a celebration of their own choice of the arts, but there is no doubt of its importance. As for the feeding of imagination, this may be more powerful in the collective context than in the individual classroom simply through the influence of numbers and the superiority of technical facilities. But two other issues are of particular importance. First, whatever may have been the case in former times, no primary school is in the same league as the daily diet of television where technical facilities are concerned. Secondly, no television channel is in the same league as the best of primary schools where the commitment of the staff is concerned. The former cannot be altered. The latter can be squandered if, in the face of sheer repetition and fatigue, the assembly and the collective life of a school becomes a chore greeted with ill-concealed cynicism or indifference, instead of allowing for an occasional dramatic climax in the school's continuity.

It requires only a slight adaptation of the wider curriculum to accommodate also the children's own aesthetic activities: the less able child's finely moulded pot, the clarinet solo at a concert, the reception class's special nativity play. Here again, so much depends on whether it is reluctantly included as a concession to seasonal or parental expectations, or whether it is a genuine expression of a school's commitment to aesthetic education.

Before looking at the last and probably the most important issue, that of values and attitudes, it is important to remember how the totality of these wider curricular activities impinges on experience. To those children whose home circumstances enable them to harmonise readily with the school's wider curriculum—and these are not necessarily the ablest, or the middle-class children, or girls, or any other group that stereotype may suggest—participation in that wider curriculum will reinforce their value to the school, and the school's value to them. To those who are less prone to respond immediately and positively, it may emphasise their lack of outstanding qualities while confirming their collective membership. They may be in the choir but not soloists, contributors to a collage but not selected for an individual painting, even perhaps a team member but not a record-breaker. Beyond these again there may be the minorities, both groups and individuals, who come to feel that their own experience prevents them from belonging in any full sense within the school community. However wide the wider curriculum may be, they still fall outside it, and its very comprehensiveness may tend to alienate them still further. For if everybody else can share it, they must be very strange to be outside it. Yet if they are tone-deaf, colour-blind, unaware of what a nativity play is, warned against taking part in this or that, and familiar instead with practices and rituals unknown to the school, then there is a strong possibility that they, and the school, will drift into a state of disengagement or 'internal exile' in which neither intrudes too far into the other.

Whether this in fact happens in any particular instances depends in the last resort on the place of values and attitudes in the wider curriculum. Here a school gathers together all the other aspects of the wider curriculum and gives them a distinctive interpretation. Two issues then become particularly significant: the actual choice of values and attitudes; and the extent to which they are consistently upheld. The actual choice is itself circumscribed by all manner of circumstantial constraints, not least among them being the need to build on a bewildering range of experience, and to secure a modicum of agreement from teachers and parents in general. It may be that by satisfying the majority, a school can intensify the difficulty for the minorities. Therefore, the case for a positive tolerance for minorities as a value in its own right is a strong one. But it is easier to tolerate, for example, a religious or ethnic minority than to tolerate a group or a subculture in which what is usually called theft or bullying is acceptable. Here, questions of moral development, community experience, individual psychology, school organisation and the fostering of values tend to fuse together. It is notoriously difficult to suggest any one general policy, even in terms of a particular religious or ethical code. As with the formal curriculum, it is also notoriously difficult to formulate those values in developmentally appropriate terms.

The other issue, that of consistency, is, in its own way, equally difficult. The more laudable and inspiring the values espoused by a school, the more difficult it is to uphold them. The very fact that teachers differ on the criteria previously mentioned: adult/child; sex/unisex; stereotype/individual: makes it all the more difficult to establish a value-consensus, especially since these criteria are compounded by all sorts of genuine differences in belief. Even individual teachers vary in their behaviour and emphasis from one day and one situation to another. Yet it is only by dint of presenting a reasonably consistent front that a school can exhibit any values and attitudes that will merit acceptance, respect or admiration, and thus sustain a wider curriculum that can enable its pupils to learn, live, choose and accept as they must. If it does do so, that can only arise from deliberate staff commitment. If it does not do so, then the permanent impact of the school on experience will be seriously diminished, and the children will remember their primary education with difficulty and indifference rather than with vividness and enthusiasm.

## Notes

1. See Parsons, T. 'The School Class as Social System' in A.H. Halsey, Jean Floud and C.A. Anderson (eds.), *Education, Economy and Society*, (Glencoe, Ill. Free Press, 1961).

2. The expression 'hidden curriculum' was probably first used by P.W. Jackson in his *Life in Classrooms*, (Holt, Rinehart & Winston, 1968). An alternative term, suggested by David Hargreaves (1978, 1982) is 'paracurriculum'.

3. Two of the best-known studies in infant schools are by Sharp and Green (1975) and by King (1978), though they differ both in nature and in ideological orientation. Studies of older primary classes include those by Nash (1973) in Scotland, and also the classic studies conducted by the ORACLE project at the University of Leicester (Galton, Simon and Croll, 1980; Galton and Simon, 1980; Simon and Willcocks, 1981; Galton and Willcocks, 1983). A somewhat different kind of ethnographic study, in Western Australia, is reported in full by Bronwyn Davies (1982). From all of these writings the significance of the hidden curriculum has to be distilled, since almost by definition it is not available for immediate inspection.

# 8 CHILDREN'S RESPONSE TO THE PRIMARY CURRICULUM

In any discussion about curriculum, especially a curriculum with claims to be an enabling curriculum, it is important to appreciate the way that the curriculum appears to children themselves. To say that a curriculum is child-centred may mean little more than that the teacher assumes that it is right for the children. It is even possible that they may go through the motions of co-operation in developing curriculum for the sake of earning an easy life through pleasing the teacher, or even through bored tolerance. And when a teacher says 'We are all interested in frog spawn this year', the reality may be that the teacher has become interested in frog spawn and that her infectious enthusiasm has spilled over effectively on to her class.

Even if it means more than that, it has to be remembered that no topic is likely to lie at the centre of the interests of every single child in a class of thirty or more. Wilson (1971) has teased out particularly clearly the complexity of the relationship between children's interests and any definable curriculum.

To pursue this point a little further, it is necessary to think again of the relation of development, experience and curriculum as already considered. Curriculum is seen as planned intervention in the interaction of development with experience. Since every child's interaction is unique, it must therefore follow that *every child's curriculum is unique, and that in a sense every child constructs his or her own curriculum.* This is of course implicit in what has already been said about the self-curriculum (p. 78 above), but the idea is worth pursuing further.

Previous chapters have treated the curriculum as though it was a unitary affair, made available as a package to at least a class and perhaps more. National curricula are of course made available to more than one class, to more than one school, in fact to a whole people. Yet whether the formal and wider curricula are devised for a class, a school or a people, and whatever variations they permit, still each individual constructs his or her own version of curriculum, and in the process evolves his or her own achieved version of the pupil's role (Calvert, 1975). And these personal curricula differ from each other in a number of ways. The most obvious of these is *performance*, which depends quite substantially on development and experience as well as on the curriculum itself. Almost equally important is what may be called *engagement*, the extent to which children are motivated or enthused or bothered by curriculum.

There is a distinction between these two. As the ORACLE studies remind us (Galton *et al*,. 1980a, 1980b; Galton and Willcocks, 1983) some good performers are able to maintain their output without giving much of themselves or, in the present terms, engaging enthusiastically with the curriculum. On the other hand, some children who engage vigorously with the curriculum simply do not perform well, like those adults who profess to like a subject while being hopeless at it. If this distinction is accepted, then a further point can be made. For if every individual child makes his or her own curriculum, then it is engagement as well as performance that is its true indication. In a curriculum with a process basis, one that emphasises skills and concepts rather than performance outputs, it becomes more defensible to emphasise the importance of engagement. At first this may seem like saying that it is better to travel hopefully than to arrive, and if a forced choice has to be made, then it is better to travel hopefully, though everyone has to arrive somewhere too, and then to move on, and on again. More important for the present discussion is the close relationship that exists between engagement and experience. To put it directly, engagement is likely to be greater where experience is more closely aligned with the formal and wider curricula of a school. That became evident in Chapter 7. It is now necessary to look at some of the same issues in the light of performance and engagement as they relate to the continuity of children's experience throughout primary education.

Evidence of children's own 'view of the curriculum' may be taken from three sources: descriptive writing about or for children, direct observations of children, and the results of empirical investigations that appear to throw some light on the question.

The last of these categories, the outcome of empirical studies, does not in fact help very much. There has been quite a long record of investigations into the relative popularity of school subjects at the primary stage, but this kind of study does not reveal anything more informative about the actual nature of the work that proved popular, or about the relation of preference choices to either performance or engagement. It seems at first sight likely that the relation with engagement would be closer than that with performance, but there is little evidence on this. More could perhaps be inferred from a close and continuous case-study such as those by Nash (1973) or Armstrong (1981), but this particular question has not usually figured in such studies.

There is a wealth of information hidden in the memories of teachers, and tersely transcribed on record cards, which does show something of the relationship between performance and engagement. However, the categories are generally poorly defined, and in any case are not specifically considered in relation to experience. There is plenty of scope for something more systematic, as will be indicated in Chapter 9, but at present the data are scanty.

Direct observation is scarcely less systematic than this. In the course of clarifying some of the ideas presented in this book, I have made a practice of checking ideas as they emerge against real children in various situations, and I hope that this precaution has in general held me back from making rash generalisations. Incidental observations of this sort can rank as evidence only in a negative, preventive sense, and it is in this way that they will be used.

There is also a third kind of evidence, a kind less usually found in what rates as professional writing about education. It includes autobiographies with vivid chapters about childhood; fictional accounts of childhood written for adults (which are often themselves thinly disguised autobiographies); and fictional accounts of childhood written for children by adults who have a talent for communicating with children. A whole volume could be written about the curriculum as it appears in these three kinds of writing, but that would require a particular kind of expertise and knowledge. However, there is clearly some value in taking the insights from such writing as a means of illuminating our understanding of children's perceptions, even if it is offset by the emphasis necessarily given to an author's own values, interests and preoccupations, and in particular to children's response to their own medium, the written word. So this kind of evidence will be sparingly used, as illustration here and there. The books referred to are listed in Appendix II. No doubt readers will wish to supplement or replace these with instances that occur to them.

It is now possible to try to erect some form of picture of how the majority of young people respond to the formal and wider curriculum, and to suggest what implications this response may have for an enabling curriculum of the kind discussed in the previous chapters. The minorities among children will be considered afterwards.

## The Formal Curriculum

Most children take their formal curriculum for granted, at least at the primary level. Development impels them to envisage primary education as an accepted process in which they are taking part, the process of being at school as part of growing up. Experience embodies their reaction. Necessarily, they think of the curriculum as being first and foremost the formal curriculum, within which they usually have little doubt about the importance of the basic skills and modes of communicating[1]. For the rest, they are likely to envisage the curriculum in terms of subject titles rather than of topics or activities, though topics and activities themselves may come to be regarded as another kind of subject: 'We did a project about that'. It is scarcely necessary to say that the enthusiasm of children for their work has little conscious relation to the curriculum theory on which it is based. Like their parents, children usually adopt quite a conventional view. They will respond to curriculum as it is, or as it changes, only if it seems in some way advantageous to do so. Fortunately for enthusiastic teachers, they do usually think it advantageous to work along with somebody who is vigorous and good fun and doesn't expect the impossible. Only years later will they be able to judge how enabling their curriculum has been.

The significance of this can be taken a step further. Children themselves see some of the curriculum in terms of their growing powers: this was noted in the discussion of growth, health and movement, and it clearly applies also to the basic skills and to others such as handling a microcomputer. Much of the rest of the curriculum, however, is perceived throughout the primary years as a series of episodes to be lived through with good-humoured tolerance and with varying degrees of engagement, rather than as a series of skills, concepts and attitudes to be acquired. They are in a sense the passengers in the aircraft. Only the pilot, the teacher, has to master the route plan and the controls. The figure of speech is not quite appropriate, because now and again some of them do glimpse something of the purpose of it all, and it is an aim of primary education that they should gradually come to perceive that purpose and gain access, so to speak, to their own flight deck, as they learn to construct their self-curriculum.

Meanwhile, the formal curriculum is likely to make differing impacts on differing groups of children. This is where the question of engagement becomes important. For most children, for most of the time, the quality of engagement is not particularly high. Sometimes there is a burst of concentrated effort, especially among the younger children[2], but when social relations develop more richly as the children grow older, the social world of the classroom acts as a distractor to all but the most single-minded and the most socially neglected children. At the same time they may develop an effective skill in peer teaching, helping their friends either in official or in illicit ways[3]. Indeed, one way of justifying ability and effort, and thus of avoiding ostracism, is to pass on one's knowledge and skill unconditionally, thereby frustrating any competitive ethos that may be officially encouraged. Teachers who prefer a co-operative ethos can here work with the grain, but have to remember that as soon as this co-operation becomes official policy, the social situation is changed. As a safety-valve, there must still be forms of co-operation that are officially discouraged but unofficially tolerated; and that then becomes a part of the organisational and hidden curricula. And needless to say there are other children in whose case it is a minor triumph for a teacher to persuade them to engage in any effort at all, even though they have considerable ability that occasionally shines through their protective armour. A case in point is that of Gowie Corby in Gene Kemp's tale of Cricklepit Combined School, *Gowie Corby Plays Chicken:*

> The morning is long and draggy and boring.
> I get half my maths wrong and have to do it again, and Miss Plum tears a page out of my English book 'cos it's so untidy, and I just can't be bothered to turn on my Tom smile. The radio programme we have on Thursdays must have been written by morons with the most awful snobby accents you've ever heard, and I get told off for drawing swastikas over my pamphlet . . .
> (p. 91)

The realism may be slightly overdone, but it is a healthy reminder of the element of negotiation that always has to intervene between teachers and children in the real world. As Jackson (1968) points out in his memorable analysis, it is by no means necessarily the case that high motivation (engagement) correlates with high performance. The recent increase of interest in classroom interaction studies betokens a willingness to concentrate on this process of negotiation. At first it may appear synonymous with capitulation on a teacher's part, a point that will be discussed further in Chapter 9.

But in fact it is a recognition of a reality that is, and must be, characteristic of all effective education, and is itself part of the society that they learn to understand. The actual way in which time is spent in a classroom or a playing field or a gymnasium is bound to involve co-operation and consent by the children as well as authority on the part of the teacher. That consent may be given grudgingly, willingly, or in sheer terror, but it has to be given. The task of the teacher is then that of ensuring that the terms of the treaty are such as to maximise the learning opportunities of the class as a whole, as the teacher sees them. But those opportunities will never reach 100 per cent, even if some theories of curriculum seem to imply that they might.

This being so, the formal curriculum negotiated with one child will involve more engagement than the formal curriculum negotiated with another child. Within the experience of any one child the negotiated curriculum will involve more engagement on one day than on another, and perhaps more in one year than in another. So each child has a profile of engagement which may, or may not, be closely associated with performance. In Chapter 9 some reference will be made to the implications of this for assessment. For now, the important consideration is how this related to the totality of experience.

On this question some clues may be drawn from retrospective comments frequently made by adults. Often these refer to specific incidents within the formal curriculum, as would be expected from the essentially concrete and episodic character of children's experience. A visit from an unusual adult, or more often a school trip to a centre such as London or York or their equivalents elsewhere, is often remembered, sometimes with a mixture of awareness of the medieval past with sing-songs in the coach on the way back. Sometimes, it must be admitted, a teacher's mistake is remembered better than a string of successes: the day when a science experiment went wrong, or when a load of coke was delivered during a hushed pause in a music broadcast. There is no easy way of telling whether the eventual learning suffered at all by reason of such disjunctions. A touch of the slapstick humour beloved of young children, however unintended, may in fact help. (So it may in secondary education).

By way of contrast with these examples of disengagement and of casual encounter, there are instances of intense curricular impact on individual children, answering some powerful interaction between development and experience in their own lives. This is another topic on which the evidence from literature throws light. In Jane Gardam's *A Long Way from Verona* one girl's poetic talent is persistently nurtured through episodes ranging from the absurd to the tragic, with the formal English curriculum playing a not insignificant part. And in the astonishing autobiography of Helen Forrester, set out in her two volumes *Twopence to Cross the Mersey* and *Liverpool Lass*[4], the feeling for language and literature first developed in a sheltered primary curriculum eventually survived an adolescence of incredible adversity, and, literally, enabled her to tell the tale. In her case it remained the one sustaining experience when development was soured and when home and environment failed: single-minded engagement leading to performance. It is understandably rarer to find similar examples embodied in literature of children for whom science or technology has proved to be the significant curricular element, though there are instances enough in which history or geography or the arts have exercised an appeal, sensitively, right from the earliest years. A public climate in which such commitment is ridiculed does not succeed in extinguishing it, but it does cause small agonies which are not revealed in studies of the sociology of the curriculum.

**The Wider Curriculum**

Children's response to the wider curriculum is at least as important. Indeed, they may regard the formal curriculum as a rather tiresome intrusion in the experience which is the wider curriculum. To some, the informal curriculum is where they come into their own. They are the stars of the teams and of the plays and clubs, the ones who stay behind after school and get to know the teachers in a more direct way, and it is incidents in the informal curriculum that they remember most vividly. They may include some who also shine in the formal curriculum; but the informal aspects are what appeal most to them, the ones within which their social relationships are forged. They have a particular developmental significance too, because these are so palpably matters appropriate for children of their age, with an evident potential for leading towards the next step. These are the activities in which their elder sister once excelled, that sister whose current preoccupation with her boyfriend is now made the subject of a mixture of mockery and awe, or in which their elder brother first learned to take the measure of school long before he became devoted to his motor-bike and his mates. There is, in fact, a wider range of engagement in the informal curriculum, with consequences for the kind of performance that is found, according to the ways in which informal activities are perceived.

Activities within the informal curriculum attract considerable attention in literary material. They range from those to whom it included elements of agony, as in Betjeman's *Summoned by Bells*, to those to whom it is a consuming passion. What is shared by the two extremes is a sense of the vividness and importance of informal activities, and in any enabling curriculum they must surely be prominent. For some children, indeed, they may provide the one moment of significance in primary education.

Closely associated with the informal curriculum is the organisational curriculum, the messages conveyed by the school as a social organisation. Usually it is seen as a centrally important matter. Its 'taken-for-granted' nature seems accepted even by truants, and in works of fiction it is usually portrayed as something to be 'sent up' and treated with light-hearted and tolerant confidence when all is going well; as a menace when there is an important test or when it is time for transfer from one stage to the next; as an intrusive nuisance in moments of high drama within the children's social world; but as a very present help in times of real trouble or terror, when even the toughest surprise themselves and everyone else by crying too. The reliable world of rules and orders is then seen to have its point, as is shown, for example, in Bernard Ashley's *Terry on the Fence*, written by an understanding author drawing on his own experience as a headmaster.

It is not just the order but the values of the school, the hidden curriculum, that are involved here. Sometimes it may engender opposition. Sometimes, however, it may express a deep concern for individuals and exemplify genuine social education in action. For example, in Tom Wakefield's *Forties Child* the author, recalling his wartime childhood, singles out the cuddling and comforting of a particularly revolting classmate by the teacher, and the challenge to accept the girl, smell and running nose and all, that the teacher directed to the author himself: 'I suppose Miss Craddock made us all a bit older—or something like that' (p. 31).

On the other hand, a latent attitude of racial prejudice can engender fierce resentment among children, though here it is necessary to remember that the prejudice may not lie entirely, or even mainly, with the teacher.

Similar issues are, of course, raised when religious or class or gender differences are involved. It is scarcely necessary to say how important they can be in influencing individual children in the extent and nature of their engagement with the curriculum. To cite instances of literature that deal with any of these aspects of the hidden curriculum would be hazardous, since there are so many of them. But this in itself emphasises something of the widespread recognition of the importance of these issues. Here again, no enabling curriculum can be adequate unless it takes them sensitively into account.

In Chapter 2 it was emphasised that children's experience, even their experience in school, is not confined to the formal and wider curriculum. There is always a part of experience that exists alongside the curriculum, and one of the latent functions of primary education is that it provides an arena within which this experience can be enacted. One of the perennial messages from school stories over the past hundred years is that the secret life of children is powerfully influential in their experience and in interaction with their development. Here, more than within the curriculum, are concentrated the episodes which arouse their attention, their effort, their excitement and anger and grief. It is as if their wider experience swamps the curriculum from time to time, like flood water after a storm[5]. This again is a common theme in literature. As the plot thickens, teachers continue woodenly to implement the curriculum, especially the formal curriculum, like some shadowy backcloth in a drama, occasionally shouting from back stage that someone is not attending, and then being fairly satisfied with an answer and fading out of experience again[6].

In fact, this experience beyond the curriculum can be interpreted as a collective alternative self-curriculum, for over the years it involves learning, in the neighbourhood but more intensely in the playground, a succession of codes and adjustments and conventional learned responses through which children complement their development with collective experience (Sluckin, 1981; Davis, 1982). It is here that pecking-orders are established and unmade, that the alleged conventional wisdom of the adult world is challenged, and that the more popular and confident individuals make their first half-ashamed, half-amused bids for heterosexual recognition.

The boundary between all this and curriculum is a real but invisible one. The ringing of a bell or the clapping of hands may be all that divides the one from the other; but everybody knows where the boundary is, and everybody except the most extreme advocates of pedagogic liberty assumes that it should be, more or less, there.

This leaves unanswered the question whether the school should officially concern itself with what happens beyond that boundary. In one sense it must: there are regular appeals through the organisational curriculum when some little procession brings a casualty to the teacher. Yet despite the existence of pastoral-care systems there may be a variety of views among the children, as well as the teachers, about how vigilant those teachers ought to be, and how far it is better to let them have their own, quite false, views about what is going on. It could be that willingness of individual children to engage in curriculum is related to what happens to them outside it.

In a boarding school, or elsewhere where social relations among children are concentrated in school with particular intensity, these issues are all the more cogent. Independent primary schools include a number of boarding schools and, while term lasts, they are total institutions. That means that the wider curriculum occupies a very large part of life, but not all of it. There is still an area of autonomy within which social relations can be worked out with all the stark directness portrayed in school stories, such as Philip Toynbee's *A School in Private*.

There, as in day schools, the impact on individuals has much to do with their family and social context, and it is easy to see this as a simple, clean form of socialisation that is a part of Life. But this cannot be assumed. The seeds of disengagement with curriculum can be sown in the seedbed of non-curricular experience, for children who do not succeed in these relationships may learn to reject the whole context with which they are associated.

## Minorities

Hitherto the child's-eye view of the curriculum has been confined to what happens within the normal stream of events in normal schools. It is important to emphasise this. For in a sense there is no such thing as an ordinary school, or ordinary children. However much they may try to be ordinary so as not to be left out of the swim, they are in fact all different. Of course, every respectable theory of the primary curriculum says that they are all different, but so often leads to actual curriculum planning that assumes that they are all, in most important respects, alike. The curriculum then comes to symbolise alikeness: this is what we do when we are all together and being alike, as distinct from what we do outside when we are all being different. Indeed, school itself often comes to symbolise the alikeness of society in its public guise. In a sense this is itself a valuable part of the organisational curriculum since it promotes social cohesion and security. Norms are more closely observed in the classroom. To cry, or swear, or be sick in class is on a par with such behaviour in church, though more immediately penalised. However, the limit of its value is reached at the point at which teachers slip into the habit of thinking that this classroom alikeness extends outside. As is often revealed in informal situations such as discos or school journeys, 'normal' children may turn out to be more enterprising, more aggressive, more original or more vulnerable than school suggests. The formal curriculum is thus revealed as a very special and protected kind of experience, and the enabling function of the wider curriculum is thus thrust into greater prominence.

There does, however, often come a point at which the semblance of normality cannot be maintained, even within the formal curriculum. Engagement may become so minimal that performance is seriously impaired. The children most prone to this disengagement are those with serious physical or mental handicaps. The sheer problem of managing themselves becomes significant, even when they are strongly encouraged to belittle their handicaps and very much want to do so. This is a central problem of the social psychology of special education, one that acquires a further urgency when children with handicaps are educated alongside others, as the 1981 Education Act advises for England and Wales. Some light is thrown on this issue by autobiographical accounts (Thomas, 1982). It is one that teachers are coming to recognise more generally, and it is impressive how much they can achieve, even when enabling is such an apparently formidable task, and how much it is appreciated when they do. Presumably the extreme case of enablement is that of Anne Sullivan's handling of Helen Keller's multiple handicaps and their social consequence: but that was not in school.

It is not easy to know how the least able children perceive the curriculum, except by inference, since they are the ones who find most difficulty in articulating their problems and are thus doubly disadvantaged. It seems likely that a personal, dependent, relationship with the teacher will be more prominent than any particular aspect of curriculum, and that therefore there is a form of engagement that can facilitate performance. Here too there is a dilemma, because the satisfaction of group membership, always rather fragile for the less able, is sometimes difficult to reconcile with the need for some element of segregation so that the teacher can make the formal aspects of an enabling curriculum more personally relevant.

The case of the emotionally disturbed children is still more difficult. Here the barrier to engagement lies precisely in the area of personal relationships. There may be some unfortunate element in the interaction of development with experience that renders curriculum as such, relatively impotent, and that also leaves the teacher encumbered with the problem of first coming to terms with this. Severe cases are of course allocated to special institutional contexts, but the facilities simply do not exist for all emotionally disturbed children to be transferred from 'normal' schools, especially when it is considered more important that they should not be taken away from other children than that they should be in the hands of specially trained teachers able, for example, to use the aesthetic aspect of curriculum diagnostically and therapeutically.

In all these instances of children with special educational needs, their own perceptions of what curriculum is about will be heavily dependent on those special needs. At the worst, it may be beyond a teacher's powers to devise for them the special curriculum that they can make their own. At the best, the need to do exactly that for them may encourage teachers to do likewise for all their pupils; but that requires outstanding quality.

There is another category of children whose perceptions of curriculum in all its aspects are now becoming a matter of concern. These are the children from minority groups, whose entire ambience in experience can dominate their pattern of engagement and thus, to a large extent, their performance also. Particular problems arise with children from strict and unusual family backgrounds who find a school's moves too lax and unstructured for their experience, or for those from permissive or structureless homes who regard school discipline with incredulity. Both set a real problem for the moral curriculum. In one sense their situation is not unlike that of the children with special educational needs: often, of course, they overlap with them.

However, the presence of ethnic minorities raises a different set of problems. The first of these, familiar to all who have worked in the field of multi-cultural education, is the danger of lumping all such groups together in a general stereotype such as 'non-native', 'immigrant', 'non-English-speaking' or (with the heavier overtones) 'coloured'. Obviously these terms do not quite overlap, and that in itself imposes some limits on stereotyping, but within each category there is great variation between groups, frequently exacerbated by conflicts elsewhere (Hindu/Moslem; Moslem/Jew; Greek/Turk, etc.) and within each group as marked individual differences as within 'normal' schools, despite apparent uniformities of dress. Yet to every one of these children the curriculum has to be related to a distinctive pattern of development and experience. Some ethnic groups do in fact show different average patterns of physical and social development when compared with the native children. All of them draw on different backgrounds of experience within which the concept of curriculum will itself occupy very different positions. For example, a Hong Kong Chinese family running a restaurant has clear expectations for, and from, its children in a way that a West Indian family headed by an unemployed second-generation immigrant may not. A whole study could be based on the different ways in which each group might envisage each of the six elements in the formal curriculum discussed in Chapter 5, not to mention the three aspects of the wider curriculum that figured in Chapter 7. Moreover, any such conjecture, however true of the 'normal' members of these groups, is likely to be wide of the mark where individuals are concerned.

Almost by definition, the aspects of the curriculum that are least familiar to all of them, and most difficult for them to engage with, are those most deeply embedded in the host culture, such as English history and English literature. Even this does not result in a uniform policy or a uniform response. From one point of view, one that is clearly represented among some of the groups concerned, the learning of such initially alien content is itself the means of acquiring acceptance and of facilitating performance. The opposite point of view is that it should be rigorously excluded, and that in its place there should be some version of Black Studies or its equivalent in other cultures. Between these two comes the 'melting pot' view, in which everyone contributes from their own culture and the sum is better than its parts. Clearly, it is not possible to follow more than one of these at once. What is less immediately clear is that to follow any of them involves substituting a social-imperatives approach for a process approach to curriculum and thereby perhaps aggravating the situation, since a social-imperatives approach draws attention to group differences, while a process approach places its emphasis on individual differences. It appears that much minority in-group opinion is in favour of a curriculum that takes account of group consciousness as such, but then such views may come from individuals particularly prone to express them. Even if this is not the case, and ethnic consciousness really is paramount in children's experience in a divided and prejudiced society, it still does not follow that the most effective curricular response is to be obtained by aligning the axis of the curriculum with that of the prejudice. In multi-cultural education many of the answers are still to be found. In finding them, the evidence from the children's patterns of engagement is still one of the most important considerations.

Similar considerations apply, though perhaps less starkly, to social class and community differences, as was indicated in Chapter 2 and also earlier in the present chapter. Much the same also characterises the children's own reactions. There is a general realisation that children do disengage from the curriculum even in the primary years. It is less certain that this disengagement is mainly on account of social-class or community differences. There are middle-class rebels and working-class aspirants, and both are likely to be articulate enough to exemplify their attitudes in writing. In almost every such case there is something in the immediate personal experience of the children or their families which proves decisive for their pattern of adjustment. Therefore, adaptation of the curriculum to ensure engagement, or for social-imperatives reasons, does not guarantee any one pattern of response. Although *Nymphs and Shepherds* are remote from the experience of many children in most environments, it is not so easy to be sure what to put in their place.

One final aspect of children's response must be remembered. The proportion of families who change house, and of children who perforce change schools, is considerable: between one-quarter and one-third, and more in some areas. For each of these there is a need for readjustment on each occasion, and sometimes there are many such occasions, for example in the case of children of members of the armed services. Any such move may entail an obligation to make a mark quickly, even brusquely, in the new community in order to assert a place in the local pecking order, or even to re-assert it after a period of absence, as Edward had to do in Penelope Lively's exquisite *Going Back*:

> On our first day back they cornered Edward in the playground.
> 'Are you with our gang then?'

And Edward, bewildered, found himself plunged into unfamiliar arrangements of alliances and enmities. The brothers had swallowed most of the school, lock, stock and barrel: either you were with them, or you were an outcast, beyond the law, a price on your head. With difficulty, he escaped them, for that day . . .
I said, 'Perhaps they'll just leave you out of things.'
'That's what girls would do.'
'Yes.' (pp. 70, 72)

They didn't; and when the fight came, Edward was not disgraced. But until it came, he had little time to think much about curriculum[7].

When children come from sharply contrasted cultural groups which, as has been pointed out, are already in a minority position, the additional problems of horizontal transition may demand a higher price, especially when the school's formal and hidden curricula operate by means that the newcomer's own culture regards as meaningless, repressive, or simply wrong. Nevertheless, after while they usually take such experiences in their stride, and gain in social maturity by doing so. Yet in the process they may lose beliefs and qualities that are not easily restored, while their intellectual development may be more seriously retarded than many people realise. In their case the need for an enabling curriculum to intervene in the interaction between development and experience and to cultivate choice and acceptance is a very real and demanding one.

There are other children who have to spend periods of their life in hospital, or ill at home, while still others absent themselves as truants or under family pressures. Systematic studies have been made of such children and their education (e.g. Oswin, 1978) and these help to ensure that they remain represented in the professional culture of teachers; necessarily so, for there are some in most schools and most classes, and they remain recalcitrant exceptions to most neat schemes of curriculum planning.

Like many other issues touched upon in the present study, this could constitute a whole important field of investigation in itself. What children think about their primary education is still only imperfectly known. Studies of the relative popularity of subjects or activities, contributions to newspaper competitions, and even close observation of children and teachers interacting in classrooms, do not fill in the whole picture. Many teachers can supplement the written word from their own experience of schools and children, but

## Children's Response to the Primary Curriculum    133

even they do not plumb the whole of the pupil's perspectives: there is almost always some element of surprise when children vouchsafe their opinions more openly than is usual. There is always more to be found out about children, however well one knows them, and teachers realise this too. They may be encouraged by realising that they, as a professional group, do emerge from all of this welter of variegated evidence in a fairly favourable light; and sometimes children think the world of them.

### Notes

1. Here and in the rest of this chapter I draw on recent informal discussions I have had with children and teachers.

2. It was one of Montessori's tenets that young children, when they had acquired mastery of a skill, would practise it oblivious of their surroundings. See A.E. George's translation (1912) entitled *The Montessori Method* (Heinemann), especially Chapter 21, and elsewhere in her writings.

3. An interesting example of peer assistance, but strictly confined to the formal curriculum, is given in Gene Kemp's superb cameo *The Turbulent Term of Tyke Tiler*. Tyke, the intelligent tomboy, helps Danny, her rather dumb protégé, to avoid being allocated to an ESN school (as they then were) by looking illegally at the test paper waiting at the headmaster's office and then coaching Danny to pass it. This he duly does; later, in hospital after an accident caused by her own daring, she confesses. Needless to say, there was a happy ending; but Tyke had shown where she stood in the scale of moral development and had almost invented a 'Consequences' test (McPhail, 1978) of her own. It is worth mentioning that this, together with its sequel *Gowie Corby Plays Chicken* referred to in Chapter 8, are among the very few examples of fiction in which an English middle school—in this case a Combined School (5-12)—figures.

4. Helen Forrester's second volume was originally entitled *Minerva's Stepchild*, after a symbol on Liverpool Town Hall. A third volume entitled *By the Waters of Liverpool* is now published (see Bibliography).

5. A sensitive study of the relation between social relations and the formal and wider curriculum at age 12-13 was made by Meyenn (1980).

6. A striking example among children just above primary age, is to be found in Jan Needle's *My Mate Shofiq*, where a tale of peer rivalries, overlain with racial conflict and ultimately tragic in its consequences, is enacted against the background of Miss Todd's valiant efforts to keep the curriculum going. She is obviously a force to be reckoned with, but the degree of engagement during episodes of crisis is minimal:

> Bernard was jerked back to the present by Miss Todd repeating his name.
> 'Bernard,' she said, sharply, 'Have you been listening? I said you can help your friend Shofiq hand out the Scripture books and collect in the pencils.'
> 'Yes, Miss, sorry Miss,' he said, looking all bright and interested. This was her soft way of giving you a treat, letting you hand out books . . .

7. The title *Going Back* does not refer to this episode but to the heroine's return to her childhood home and the memories it recalls.

# 9 TEACHERS FOR AN ENABLING CURRICULUM

There can be no curriculum without teachers. Indeed, Alexander (forthcoming) claims that the primary curriculum cannot be considered apart from primary teachers. Certainly, an enabling curriculum is bound to require a distinctive approach from teachers: not necessarily greater demands, but a willingness to think in terms of the development and experience of individual children, to plan curriculum as intervention, and to consider equipping children for choice and for acceptance.

It is not only necessary for teachers to consider curriculum in the light of children's development and experience. They have also to take account of their own development and experience. They too are on a series of curves of development, physical, intellectual and social/emotional, which powerfully affect their own powers and procedures. Inevitably, different teachers are at different points on those curves. Even in primary schools the youngest teachers are nearer in chronological age to their youngest pupils than they are to their oldest colleagues. In the extreme case they may be at the pinnacle of achievement in a sport which is only a memory and a clutch of trophies to their colleague in the next classroom. In intellectual terms the younger staff may retain a flexibility of mind that acts as a counterpoint to the accumulated wisdom of the older staff. In personal terms heads nearing the end of their careers may well think of the youngest staff as, professionally, their children or even their grandchildren. Their own sons and daughters may well be considerably older than their youngest colleagues.

Quite apart from these age-differences, individual teachers change as time passes. Their patterns of relationships with colleagues and children undergo modifications as they become less physically vigorous but more generally mature, and it requires regular vigilance to ensure that an individual teacher remains aware of these changes and of their consequences. Through consistent cultivation of awareness of their own development, they become more sensitive to developmental considerations among children.

It is equally important for teachers to appreciate the significance of their own experience. In one sense this is always recognised: there is general respect for 'experienced' teachers both in selection for posts of responsibility and in recruitment for teacher education.

At the same time there is widespread suspicion about teachers' lack of experience of life in general. In considering an enabling curriculum, teachers need to be aware of both these characteristics, and also to build on their experience of children to extend their own understanding of development and experience in children. In fact, any teacher gains in experience simply by dint of working with children, and gains in quality of experience by reacting sensitively to the development and experience of children. The appraisal and assessment of pupils, one activity which will shortly be discussed, is a process which becomes both easier and more accurate because it has been done before, though at the same time there is a risk that the teacher, either through personal development or experience, may alter the norm of assessment without being aware of doing so. Also, with the passage of time, there may be real differences between, say, 6-year-olds in 1980 and 6-year-olds in 1985. The difficult point to grasp and to bear regularly in mind is that the entire teaching-learning complex—pupils, teachers, curriculum, and cultural context—is changing all the time. None of us can stop the world.

There is another form of experience that has also to be borne in mind. Professional training was a very different matter when the older teachers were in college. The sequence of professional experience that, in England and Wales, leads from an Ordinary BEd. or an Open University degree to an Honours degree, or a Diploma, and then perhaps an MEd., or from a degree and Postgraduate Certificate in Education (PGCE) on to the same path, is very different from the two- or three-year Certificate course which was formerly considered adequate and self-contained, requiring only occasional supplementation with a refresher course or two as—in a significant phrase—'post-experience' training. To teachers from the more recent patterns of training, the expectation of professional growth is much more in-built.

Thus, teachers at different points on their curves of development will not only have different extents and kinds of experience. They are likely also to be differently equipped to understand and take account of the development and experience of children. This is bound to affect their general readiness to consider curriculum as planned intervention in the interaction between development and experience, though many individuals in both patterns of professional training will stand out as exceptions.

When we think of how teachers as a whole figure in relation to an

## 136 Teachers for an Enabling Curriculum

enabling curriculum, a number of considerations present themselves. Some of the most prominent are these:

> Are some teachers more suited than others to develop an enabling curriculum?
> What kinds of equipment do teachers need in order to develop it?
> What changes in teachers' role are implied if it is to be developed?
> What co-operation can teachers look for among adults in developing it?

and in a different vein:

> What are the implications for the initial and in-service education of teachers if an enabling curriculum is to be developed?

In the remainder of this chapter with particular reference to primary teachers in England and Wales, these issues will be examined in turn.

The first issue is as complex as it is important, and the literature relevant to it is immense. For a long time it was thought that research might reveal which people were likely to become good teachers of any kind, until it became evident that they were many kinds of teaching, and many kinds of person, and no simple definition of good teaching, even though it is fairly easy to recognise at least some forms of bad teaching. More recently, attention has come to be focused on particular styles of teaching or particular principles of procedure, and also on the social origins and experience of particular teachers and their congruence with particular categories of children. To take this last point first, there is some reason to think that the most appropriate teacher to understand and enable working-class children, or rural children, would be a teacher from their own background; and similarly for other situations. In fact, there is little consistent evidence to that effect.

Similar considerations apply to the processes of pedagogy. These are skills that can be taught and learned in teacher education, as Stones (1979) has advocated. They are related to individual acts of teaching and learning that can figure in any structure of curriculum, and can improve teaching within it. This being so, they are important in any teacher education, including preparation for an enabling curriculum. But they are not strictly linked to that curriculum.

If neither social origins nor pedagogic skill is directly associated with suitability to enact an enabling curriculum, might it at least be true that some teaching styles are more appropriate than others for this purpose? The two principal studies of infant schools in England (Sharp and Green, 1975; King, 1978) do not show a consistent pattern of evidence on this theme, though they do indicate its potential importance. Bennett's (1976) study was of course directly focused on teaching styles, this time in junior schools, and in the interaction between variables analysed in his study there was a distinct advance in knowledge about the effect of a range of teaching styles. However, the main dependent variable was an objective measurement of attainment, which is rather a different matter from the implementation of a particular pattern of curriculum. The ORACLE[1] team at Leicester carried this type of analysis a stage further (Galton, Simon and Croll, 1980; Galton and Simon, 1980), bringing out the interactions between styles of teaching and styles of learning, but here too the measure selected was attainment. The most directly relevant findings of the ORACLE studies in relation to an enabling curriculum were probably those concerning the outcomes of class teaching. For it was demonstrated that the class-teaching pattern allowed more direct pupil-teacher interaction than was possible through 'individual monitoring' of pupils working on their own, so that, paradoxically, a curriculum that aims to cater for individual needs may do so more effectively when some teaching, particularly of subject-areas depending on sequential skill and concept formation, is done collectively. This is not to be taken as an inflexible paradigm across the curriculum. In the ORACLE studies particular attention was paid to language and mathematical and scientific skills, and it could well be that a combination of individual and group study would be more suitable for some topic work in the social subjects. Again, there is probably a legitimate contrast between the teaching of skills in art and craft and of those required in music. In addition, any individual teacher is likely to find a particular mix of styles most appropriate for himself or herself. The criterion of appropriateness here may be more than measurable efficiency, for it could be maintained, for example, that the social experience derived from group work, suitably and sensitively handled, is more important than any outcome measured in terms of performance alone.

It is possible here only to hint at some of the implications of

Bennett's studies and the ORACLE publications for an enabling curriculum in primary education; and to emphasise the point that they have both made, namely, that these issues are more complex than protagonists of either 'traditional' or 'progressive' opinions have always allowed.

In general terms, then, it appears that the social origins of teachers and their actual pedagogic acts are not directly associated with any particular approach to curriculum. Teaching styles may have some relevance, though it is more a question of finding the right mix than of opting for any one style.

There still remains the possibility that teachers' personalities, motivations, characters or values might have a direct relationship with the development of an enabling curriculum. It is still more difficult to appeal to research findings for this purpose. Ashton's study of aims in primary education (Ashton et al., 1975) provides a baseline for any such investigation, but its main thrust is the relationship between particular categories of teacher, values and emphases in curriculum and other variables. If anything, it would indicate that teachers who are younger and equipped with a more sophisticated professional preparation would be likely to look more favourably on a process approach. Bassey's survey within one county (Bassey, 1978) portrays graphically what teachers in primary schools actually do, but does not penetrate beyond this. Neither of these studies would claim to indicate more than trends to which there are many exceptions, or to postulate that opinion as measured at the time of their studies is not liable to alteration. Indeed Ashton (1981) has explicitly pointed out what changes may be taking place. Beyond this it would probably be legitimate to say that teachers with authoritarian tendencies, or with a penchant for hierarchical organisation, for dogmatic statements and enforced compliance, would not be well suited to implement an enabling curriculum; but then they would not want to. Difficulties would arise only if somebody else, applying their own methods to a different value-position, said that they had to. Such a situation is not unknown in primary education, and indeed it may be worsened if it results from an innovation introduced brusquely and without adequate consultation. For the real necessity in the development of an enabling curriculum is the commitment of the teachers concerned to a value-system consonant with its implications. In most other respects the qualities that make good teachers in a forms-of-understanding approach or a social-imperatives approach are likely to make good teachers in a process approach. In teaching styles there may be some differences. In values and commitment, the difference is crucial.

On the assumption that suitable teachers are available in suitable numbers, it is next necessary to consider what kinds of equipment they need in order to implement an enabling curriculum. For this purpose it may be useful to look at the five elements in the armour of primary teachers designated in the report of postgraduate certificate courses for teachers in primary and middle schools (UCET, 1982). They apply to primary teachers irrespective of their pattern of training. The first of these is what may be broadly described as 'technique', that is, the indispensable skills of classroom organisation and procedure. The next two require more specific comment.

One of these is curricular knowledge, including knowledge about the concept of curriculum as discussed in Chapter 3, but also sufficient knowledge of an appropriate kind about the main components of any curriculum, including those discussed in Chapters 5 and 6 as they apply to an enabling curriculum. The sheer quality of expertise that is potentially required for one teacher to mediate the curriculum discussed in those chapters is daunting, and must in practice result, at least in the upper primary years, in some form of sharing of function. Even so, a team of teachers can only just manage to cover the range of expertise in skills and familiarisation that is necessary. It must be noted that this is not a range of knowledge, for a process approach does not basically require the transfer of knowledge from teachers to children. What is required is a way of transmitting skills and concepts and attitudes. There are procedures appropriate to mathematics, to science, to art, to PE and to each other aspect of curriculum, and these are not mere concessions to the forms-of-understanding approach. The sharpening of perceptions itself depends on disciplined observation and deduction. No enthusiasm for discovery will in itself lead a teacher for example to recognise the relationship between rock type, soil and vegetation, or to place a local building in the social totality of its historic period, or to know how to evaluate the quality or significance of a child's artistic or musical invention. And if the teacher is unaware, then the quality of the curricular experience for the child is thereby diminished. It would be unrealistic to imagine that any but the most exceptional of teachers can do other than accumulate, through their own experience, some equipment of this kind and to share it with colleagues, learning meanwhile from them and from others.

Alongside curricular knowledge must be reckoned professional knowledge. This is the necessary cornerstone of an enabling curriculum, for it is through professional knowledge that a teacher is able to analyse development, experience, and their relation to curriculum. It involves familiarisation with the kinds of thinking discussed in the preceding chapters as well as with other approaches to the understanding of children in schools. It also means rather more than that, for it implies a readiness to practise curriculum design and implementation with development and experience in mind. Since each child's development and experience is unique, it might seem at first sight logically necessary to design a special curriculum for each child as planned intervention in his particular development and experience, and to keep doing so as he and his experience continue to change. Plainly, that would be absurd; yet the only practicable alternative is to enact some kind of compromise which is reasonably on-target for a class, and then to monitor each individual's progress through the common experience. It is in fact justifiable to do this, since one facet of an enabling curriculum is that it shall have common features and enable children to grow up and live together. This compromise has then to be negotiated with a class in order to secure their continuing engagement at a reasonable level, a procedure that implies not surrender but constructive realism.

If a teacher has an idea about the development and experience of a child, or the children living together in class, this implies also some notion about how learning takes place. It involves knowing how to assess progress in respect of curricular experience in different aspects of curriculum[2], and how to diagnose, in the process, what children are capable of doing next. This is a procedure often to be identified in practice, ranging from the infant teacher's 'Why don't you make me a big one, and don't forget his ears?' to the suggestion made to children in a junior or middle school: 'You two go over there and try it again, and weigh what is left over'. In a broad sense each new venture is then assessed in its turn, and eventually it becomes possible to build up a cumulative record such as Clift, Weiner and Wilson (1981) advocate. In each individual learning episode this requires sensitivity about the whole process, including awareness that in each child, in each aspect of the curriculum, the profiles both of performance and of engagement are likely to be irregular, and the relation between performance and engagement, unpredictable. The skill needed to achieve this degree of sensitivity and awareness requires not only a grasp of the ways in which learning actually takes place, but a readiness to match the assessment to the learning[3]. This is more straightforward to undertake in the sequential, skill-based aspects of curriculum, such as mathematical understanding, than in those whose structure is more open and problematical.

The remaining two elements in a primary teacher's equipment are of a more personal nature. One is in fact the set of personal and interpersonal skills and qualities that are needed in a teacher when relating to children and indeed to other adults too. These skills and qualities include sensitive facility in matters such as the grouping of children, the possibilities of peer teaching, and indeed the organisational curriculum itself. Partly these arise from professional knowledge, but partly also from personality and character and from a teacher's own experience and the sustained habit of self-analysis. In the complex and varied organisation of a class for different purposes, it demands almost a form of intuition, which the ablest of teachers of young children seem to show, but which is actually built up through prolonged insight into the development and experience of children. The remaining element, hinted at in the discussion of personal qualities, is that of constant critical appraisal of oneself, one's aims, and one's context and outcome of action. Provided that it does not become discouraging on the one hand, or a form of self-indulgence on the other, criticism of this kind leads to the continuous readjustments that a truly enabling curriculum requires. Awareness of the hidden curriculum is particularly important here.

The consequence of maintaining these five elements (technique, curricular knowledge, professional knowledge, personal and interpersonal relationships, critical appraisal) is that the role-complex of teachers becomes widened and the task itself of a higher professional standing. In addition to the usual roles of instructor, classifier, socialiser etc. (Blyth, 1965) and the more fully elaborated analyses presented by Hoyle (1969), Musgrove and Taylor (1969) and Grace (1972), an enabling curriculum requires at least three others. One is that of the teacher as *researcher*, as advocated by Stenhouse (1975). By the mastery of procedures of systematic observation and recording, even in the most rudimentary way that is all that time permits, a teacher is able to combine the use of professional knowledge with the demands of interpersonal relations and the need for critical appraisal. Being research-minded does not mean putting on a metaphorical white coat and distancing oneself from children. It resembles far more the situation of the medical man whose research orientation sharpens his diagnosis and medication. Where it is possible, a whole range of new-wave techniques of observation and evaluation can be learned and applied, but it is the orientation, the attitude, that matters; that of learning from and in the teaching situation rather than taking oneself and one's knowledge and skills as an invariant datum. In one of his later papers Stenhouse (1980) linked the teacher's research role with that of the artist, thus imparting a new dimension to it.

The second additional role (the third will be considered later) is that of *team member*. This is an almost inevitable consequence of the expansion of curricular and professional knowledge. It has already become obvious that no one teacher can master all the skills, concepts and procedures that are needed in an enabling curriculum. But if there is to be sharing, it does not take place automatically. For one thing there may not be an exact match between curricular needs and teacher competences. There may be too many geographers and too few physical scientists; a gaggle of guitarists and no pianist. In that case, a team has to look for some kind of adjustment, which in effect means either dispensing with something important for the curriculum, or seeing that somebody develops an additional expertise. Readiness to take this role has not always been characteristic of primary teachers. What is more, the newly acquired expertise—or any other expertise for that matter—may be in the hands of a junior member of staff who has to learn the skill of advising much more established teachers, while they in turn have to learn the harder skill of being advised by a slip of a girl, or a young fellow not five minutes out of college, or however it may be put. Yet this is the implication of staff development of this kind. It involves a kind of *professional status-inversion* (Blyth and Derricott, 1977), but it is a necessary step towards the other role of curriculum consultant that is advocated for this reason in the HMI survey of 1978 (DES, 1978).

In the remainder of this chapter attention will be given to some of the ways which schools and teachers can move towards the personnel, equipment and roles required for the implementation of an enabling curriculum.

**School-based Innovation**

First, it is necessary to mention briefly the kinds of development that can take place within a school. Basically, these must be designed and implemented by the head of a school, together with a nucleus of enthusiastic colleagues who may or may not be among the senior members of staff[4].

This is in itself a delicate operation, for it implies that the head must exercise a dual role, that of leader and also that of innovator. He or she must be equipped for both, and confident in an ability to discharge both. And the innovation is not only a curricular innovation, but rather an innovation in organisational climate and procedures intended to facilitate a continuing series of curricular innovations which themselves have implications for the wider curriculum. It involves getting senior and junior colleagues to accept a situation in which there will be continuing demands on professional knowledge, professional skills and curricular knowledge, and the possibility of increasing and threatening conflicts in values between colleagues. Almost by definition it is a situation calculated to increase rather than to decrease uncertainty. Dewey once spoke of the need to substitute security of procedure for security of belief; but this is a case where security of procedure is itself the casualty, until a new kind of procedure is substituted. In an age in which an emphasis on either development or experience is frequently blamed for every cognitive and moral defect in the body politic, a transition within a school to a new way of looking at curriculum is likely to be still more difficult. Yet without it, any serious attempt to rethink the primary curriculum in detail must be at risk. At best it will influence two or three members of staff, who will continue to support each other until one of them leaves, after which the whole process may well falter and fail. At worst, the whole process of curriculum change may be frozen out at the start, the reason given being that it is a high-sounding theoretical idea with no practical significance, whereupon everyone heaves a sigh of relief and goes on just as before.

If the school is a very small one, a different set of problems may arise (Brown and Turnock, 1981). There is no doubt a considerable value in the small, familial institution, but the demands of curricular knowledge and professional knowledge fall disproportionately on small schools, and ironically it may happen that the very efforts needed in order to make an innovation effective will cause greater strains than in a larger school which is already better equipped in terms of range of expertise and personnel. In an age of declining school rolls in so many countries the small-school problem is not itself declining, even when it is held at bay by amalgamations (which bring other strains of their own). So this small-school problem is not likely to disappear. Meanwhile, there is even more bitter irony in the contrast that those countries with growing populations and greater numbers clamouring for primary education are just those which cannot yet afford to resource an enabling curriculum at all.

Of course, in this as in most other forms of innovation, case-studies of successful initiatives provide the best evidence. These can then be used to convince others. 'Show me!' is a very understandable demand, and it should be increasingly met by those who have shown themselves what can be done.

**Support Agencies**

Even for this purpose it is necessary to provide some effective support. The twin aspects of the researcher role, that of closer observation of children and that of enterprising experiments with formal and wider curriculum, both call for professional support beyond the resources of individual schools. Fortunately, they can be supplied by different agencies. This indicates the patterns of in-service provision that are required.

The first is concerned with the refinement of professional skills. This could well be entrusted to two kinds of agency. One is the personnel skilled in this field that are to be found in Universities, Polytechnics and Colleges of Higher Education. The practical difficulty in such matters is always that of deploying the resources of time, manpower, and money in a mutually satisfactory way. At the same time there is a different problem, that of rendering outside experts and school staff mutually acceptable. There is always the danger that both 'sides', at their own stages of professional development and experience, will stereotype the other, the personnel from higher education tending to think of the school staff as context-bound and perhaps lacking in perspective, while the staff regale each other with despairing comments about the jargon-ridden approach of their counterparts, and perhaps with lurid conjectures about how they would manage the most troublesome of the 9-year-old classes. Yet this too is a phase that can be transcended by experience based on a combined approach to curricular problems, provided that both 'sides' interact regularly with the children and genuinely value the development and experience of the other.

The other potential agency is the advisory service of the local education authorities. Here too there is a role-problem, but it is rather a different one. There may still be some suspicion of those with a lack of demonstrable recent classroom experience, but it is sometimes overshadowed by the dual role of advisors, for they are also seen as inquisitors bent on facilitating accountability. Here too collective experience can fairly soon reduce suspicions, but this requires time, which is often desperately short for both partners.

In view of the long and increasingly successful partnership that has been built up between parents and teachers, it is evident that the help of parents can be drawn upon in several ways. First, their own knowledge of their children and of their neighbours' children, especially at the infant stage, is a positive asset. If they can be persuaded that a curriculum is really intended to enable their children and not to subject them to some current fad, they can play a number of valuable roles. They and their extended families can figure also as experts in particular fields. Their development and experience can also be drawn on, and in the case of the unemployed and the retired, it may help to give significance to their own lives if they are invited to contribute from their expertise, their concerns and their memories (see Chapter 7). Families can also help particularly in the informal curriculum, when resources permit, by lending a hand in the planning and execution of journeys and visits which can make a powerful impact on the experience of children. Finally, the involvement of families can have a direct outcome because it gives them dignity and significance in front of their children and their children's friends, and contributes to the organisational curriculum by presenting the school in relation to the community, and to the hidden curriculum by combating value-differences between home and school.

Meanwhile there is another kind of support that may be required, in curricular knowledge itself. It is the more enterprising experts in different academic disciplines who can best help here: natural scientists, historians, geographers, social scientists—as well as those devoted to different kinds of artistic activity, and also the representatives of various aspects of political, economic, social and religious life. All of these could enrich the resources available to teachers, but it is difficult indeed to effect the necessary liaison. For one thing, unless their institution has been actively involved in the education of the young (as in the case of institutions of higher education with a tradition in teacher education) there is a lack of the basic mechanisms by which the experts can be brought together with the teachers. Casual social acquaintance is one possible means of contact: team games, golf, chess and bridge have all been known to play a part in establishing such links, as have common membership of churches and of political parties, or simply chats over the garden fence. There may even be some positive virtue in what is just done 'for a pal', except that for each school such opportunities are left very much to chance. Even where they are effected, there can be problems. The Schools Council Industry Project, with whose activities for younger children I have been involved[5], has often encountered the problem of how to persuade personnel managers and sales representatives that the style required in primary schools is rather different from their customary forms of discourse. Here again, however, there is scope for experience to bring the participants together, and possibly it should be a part of the evolving role of heads to become facilitators of the participation of other adults in schools.

All of these suggestions may, of course, seem rather Utopian in terms both of resource allocation and of social reality. It requires a Plato or an Illich to envisage a troupe of scholars, research chemists, ballet dancers, car salesmen and representatives of British Rail holding themselves in readiness for a phone call from St Mary's or Acacia Avenue, even if they did know what to do when they arrived. In any case they can be released only occasionally for such purposes, however favourably they may regard them. In addition there can be hidden conflicts, particularly where power and identity are under potential threat. An industrial enterprise is unlikely to open up its industrial relations to intrepid questioning from Sandra, aged 7, nor is a professional historian likely to welcome being asked to make a contribution to what he perceives as something perfunctorily and uncomprehendingly termed Environmental Studies. Still less is a member of a local bureaucracy likely to submit to the sort of interrogation from primary pupils that he contrives to avoid in more public situations; and if this is done, it only gives a false and cosy impression of social realities.

All of these considerations have to be borne in mind by teachers and especially head teachers as they draw on the repertoire of potential support. They in turn constitute a form of professional experience whose acquisition is a challenge, which can result in a third addition to the role-complex of primary teachers, that of *community relations facilitator*.

Alongside these developments there is a place for more systematic professional enhancement through courses for named qualifications. Open University degrees in Educational Studies are a case in point. Further, the analysis of development and of experience could figure valuably in Diploma, BPhil and MEd. courses, or their equivalents, which customarily include a component of more rigorous empirical study. Where Honours BEd. courses are required to involve studies in Education and one other discipline, as is often the case, this combination is particularly well suited to a case-study of a teacher's own class embarking on something new related to the student's other main discipline. However, it would be self-defeating if every teacher were to feel it obligatory to undertake such sustained study for a named qualification. This is only one way in which collective professional experience can be enhanced, and one that should be neither belittled nor given exaggerated importance in a teacher's career profile. The principal value to a school of having on its staff one or two members who are engaged in disciplined study of this kind is that they can, and increasingly do, act as translators of educational scholarship and research, and thus as a means of bringing their colleagues more effectively into the wider discourse of the teaching profession as a whole. This too involves a process of professional experience in which they personally may be open to the same suspicions that can attach to their mentors, but which they can learn to overcome. Incidentally, there is much to be said for introducing into courses of advanced study at least some guidance in the handling of these colleague relationships, as a necessary step towards the establishment of effective curriculum planning.

At an earlier stage in the discussion it was suggested that schools in the present circumstances may manifest a situation in which the most senior members of the staff were trained in an age in which subsequent professional development was not regarded as important when compared with the virtues of experience, while the younger ones have been educated with the opposite assumption. It is this kind of situation that is caricatured in the story of the head who basked in the security of thirty years' experience, which his irreverent colleagues preferred to regard as one year's experience, repeated thirty times. This is where professional status-inversion may arise. Ironically, the more effective the programme of post-experience and advanced study, the greater the likelihood that this professional status-inversion will emerge. The courses themselves should, therefore, also include some reference to coping strategies for this purpose.

## Initial Teacher Education

In the longer run, however, the main determinant of change in schools is the pattern of initial teacher education. If the teaching profession is to be increasingly equipped with teachers capable of planning an enabling curriculum as interaction between development and experience in the lives of children which can equip them for choice and acceptance, then it follows that their courses of initial training have to prepare them for this task. There is, of course, no need and no room for such considerations to be added to an already full programme. Therefore, the existing programme has to be used, and if necessary modified, for this purpose. It is worth while to look briefly at the way in which the necessary competence in studies of development, experience and curriculum can be fostered, and to consider how far this might involve modifying the usual pattern of course.

First, unlike teachers on post-experience courses, students in initial training are all at more or less the same point in professional development, and often in the same early-adult phase of general development too. They have thus reached a point at which it becomes possible to consider their own development with a little more insight and objectivity than is usually possible during adolescence, and to learn to transcend any tendency to stereotype that they may have. They have also probably been able to observe the development of relatives and friends, to read more widely, and to begin to make valid generalisations from personal experience, to be set against the background of what they read in the professional literature. At the same time, and for similar reasons, they can also formulate opinions about their own experience and that of others, and to distinguish experience from development. This capacity can be fostered by general information about child development and social background. It is quite usual to include in a course of this kind some form of Child Study, and this appears a very suitable way of focusing attention on what development and experience mean in an individual child. It can also be enriched by some study of the child's cultural context, for as Bernstein insisted, teachers must first be acquainted with this, if they are to enable children to grow toward their own culture. But a closer analysis of development and experience in relation to curriculum is also needed. This could be a separate requirement or a prescribed part of the basic exercise itself, with an obligation to consider the implications of development and experience in that child's life for his or her curriculum. It would then be interesting to match the student's interpretation of what is desirable with the actual curricular sequence encountered by the child, and to reflect on the outcome.

So far, these requirements would involve only a slight modification in what is widespread practice at least in BEd. courses: the PGCE may allow less scope, but it should not therefore be assumed that this is impossible or unimportant (UCET, 1982). The next step is a little less usual: it involves looking at examples of other children's development and experience on the lines indicated in Chapter 8. Children in fiction and autobiography, carefully selected, can reveal the relationship between development, experience and curriculum vividly, and one or two seminars based on the comparison between dissimilar child careers could quite quickly bring out some of the main issues, which could be further examined through direct observation in the course of the work in schools which is likely to constitute an increasingly important part of BEd. and PGCE courses.

Finally, due emphasis could be placed on the significance of development and experience in each piece of curriculum planning in which the students take part, individually or collectively, in concert with teachers or otherwise.

Where it is possible to make some form of IT-INSET link (Ashton *et al.*, 1982), and thus to lay emphasis on the importance of development and experience simultaneously in the education of new and of experienced teachers, the advantages may be considerable. Attitudes in the collaborating schools may thus be changed at the time that the new teachers' attitudes are being formed, while the resources of the 'training institutions' could be more readily made available to the schools in these circumstances.

Of course, this emphasis on development and experience as major considerations and on curriculum in relation to them should not be made at the expense of other concerns. That would not be necessary. In fact, to organise much of the philosophical, psychological, sociological and curricular content of a course in this way could well result in an actual saving of time and a sense of direction in the work itself.

### Research

In this chapter attention has been focused on the changes in the teacher's role that are implied in an enabling curriculum involving planned intervention in the interaction between development and experience, and on the procedures needed to bring about such changes. In the course of examining these changes in the teacher's role, the need for a 'research' orientation was emphasised, but this was described as an attitude rather than a technical activity. In conclusion, however, it must be emphasised that there is an important, even an essential, place for specific and rigorous research to expose and extend the implications of the approach to curriculum suggested here. For example:

(1) There could be longitudinal case-studies of the responses of individual classes and of individual children to curriculum in the light of development and experience. These would be difficult enough to conceptualise, still more to conduct, but without them the whole argument must remain to some extent speculative.
(2) There could be other studies of children's experience, by a variety of means: observation, interview, projection and other ethnographic techniques. These might be sensitively extended to an examination of the meaning of children's experience to themselves. We have much still to learn about development; but we probably have more still to learn about experience.
(3) There is much scope for studies of methods of pupil assessment appropriate to this approach to curriculum, and in particular those methods which relate to the aesthetic aspects of the curriculum and to the understanding of the natural and social world.

These are only a few of the fields which could be effectively investigated. What brings these together is that all of them can, technically, be carried out by a teacher with appropriate training and skills and interest in the course of working in a primary school. Some indication of these possibilities has already been mentioned in connection with diploma and higher-degree work, and it is increasingly recognised that among primary teachers, including infant teachers, there are a number who show in their previous studies that they have the ability to undertake work of this kind without detriment to their basic teaching role. This is as it should be. In any profession research should be substantially in the hands of the practitioners. In that way the role of research is itself more effectively maintained. For research of this kind is likely to keep to the middle road between undue subordination to instrumental needs on the one hand, and divorce from 'relevance' on the other. Research of this kind is most likely to permeate the professional consciousness and to lead eventually to the modification of practice: in this case, to the further modification of the teacher's role. Indeed, through exercise of critical appraisal, research might intervene in the interaction between their own continuing development and experience and lead them in the light of their own basic values to amend, transcend or reject the concept of an enabling curriculum itself. They would then, and only then, be entitled to do so. In which case, being entitled, they should not hesitate to do so.

## Notes

(1) ORACLE stands for Observation, Research And Classroom Learning Evaluation. This major project on learning in primary schools, directed by Professors Brian Simon and Maurice Galton at the University of Leicester, has resulted in four major publications (Galton *et al.*, 1980a, 1980b; Simon and Willcocks 1981; Galton and Willcocks (eds), (1983), all of which are referred to elsewhere in the present volume.

(2) Some interesting developments in assessment have been evolved by Harlen (1977) in primary science, Tough (1977a, 1979) in language, and Cooper (1976) in the social subjects. A more wide-ranging programme by the Assessment of Performance Unit has in practice contributed to assessment of development in language, mathematics and science while noting the problems of doing so in physical, aesthetic and personal/social development. At the secondary level the volume of work is much greater and some of it has considerable significance for the primary years. There is generally an increasing tendency to emphasise profile assessment of skills and concepts. For a general survey, see Shipman (1983).

(3) At the time of writing I am engaged in a small-scale study of assessment of children's social knowledge and awareness at the age of transfer between primary and secondary education.

(4) An interesting instance of innovation on these lines in a middle school is given by Johnston (1981). See also pp. 96–7 above.

(5) The outcome of a series of small-scale initiatives in Industry Education with younger children will probably be published by the Industry Project. See p. 98, note 4, above.

# 10 AN ENABLING CURRICULUM IN PERSPECTIVE

Throughout the preceding discussion it has been taken for granted that primary education is a relatively established stage in the personal history of children. It is a stage that is defined, in most societies, by the age-span 6 to 12 or thereabouts, though in England and Wales it has for historical reasons extended, in most cases, from 5 to 11. Within that stage it has also been assumed that primary schooling occupies, generally, a central place in the lives of children, so that even when they sit lightly to it, school is where they live for much of their time, and school is the nub of their experience. Hitherto, again, little has been said about what happens when primary education is finished. In this final chapter these issues will be more closely examined, and their implications for development and experience and an enabling curriculum in its formal and its wider aspects considered. For it is within this context that any specific planning must take place.

The age-boundaries are relatively easy to consider. In any one political unit there is a temptation to assume that the age-range then in force has some kind of sanction in Nature. This is never so. The very fact that systems differ itself indicates that no one age-range is necessarily right. Certainly, the English 5-7-11 pattern, largely based on the need for separate infant schools in the specific circumstances of early industrial society and on the later introduction of 'secondary education for all', must by its separateness stand as proof that the primary age-range is man-made. In addition, English independent schools, especially boys' schools, have always operated on a different age-scale, while in the past twenty years the reconsideration of 'ages and stages' has been specifically advocated in the Plowden Report (CACE, 1967) and spasmodically implemented in those areas where middle schools have been established. Elsewhere in the West, except in Scandinavia, a 6-12 age-span following a pre-school period is usual. Scotland shares the upper, though not the lower, limit of this majority Western pattern. Meanwhile, in the Communist world, where transfer from pre-school is usually postponed until 7, the separateness of a primary stage itself is less marked. In much of the Third World, primary education is still what Europe and North America used to regard as elementary education, the only education that most of the population ever received.

Age-ranges themselves do not drastically alter the way in which an enabling curriculum interacts with development and experience. However, the addition of one year, 11-12, to the normal English pattern does permit a positive expansion of both intellectual and social development, so that those middle schools which have been able to retain their morale and resources have shown a notable extension in what can be achieved in all aspects of the formal and informal curriculum, while retaining the positive features of the organisational and hidden curriculum characteristic of primary schools. This is a bald generalisation without tight empirical support, but it corresponds with the impressions of many who teach in these schools, especially where they have not been severely affected by reductions in resources. Middle schools that cater for children aged 9-13 in England, or 10-14 in the USA show further changes which in the latter case involve the development of a culture more centred on early adolescence. Nevertheless, they are able to sustain an enabling curriculum of the kind outlined in the preceding chapters in a way that a secondary or high school would find considerably more difficult.

**Transition**

Consideration of the age-ranges of primary education involves also some appraisal of what takes place when primary education comes to an end. Recently, attention has come to be focused increasingly on the process of transfer from one stage to the next, and there is sufficient evidence about this transfer in England to warrant some informed comment. Much of the discussion has centred round curricular continuity, so that the evidence is particularly pertinent to the formal curriculum.

The major change is from a class-teacher to a subject-teacher organisation. This is also accompanied by a change from a curriculum in which the process approach is most evident, to one which forms of understanding predominate. Later in secondary education there may be more evidence of the social-imperatives approach, but at first it is the move towards subjects that stands out in virtually all of the major studies such as those by Nash (1973), Youngman (1978), Bryan (1980) and the recent and very important ORACLE research on transfer from junior (and middle) schools (Galton and

Willcocks, 1983). Ignoring for the moment the social significance of transfer, the effect of a subject-based curriculum going beyond forms of understanding is to show marked disjunction with primary work, one which can bring about a relative deterioration in the engagement and performance of some children and at the same time, though the stimulus of new surroundings and new activities can have the opposite effect on others. Some secondary schools do, as a matter of policy, make a point of continuing something of a process approach in their first year so that an enabling curriculum could be prolonged quite effectively; and this is particularly true in English, the creative arts and in some aspects of science and social studies. Since the immediate purpose for which enablement aims is that of equipping children for work in the secondary school, this first-year provision constitutes a beneficial feature of transition, especially when it is facilitated by planned co-operation between the staffs of the different schools. It can and should be also a way of taking account of rapid changes in the children's development and experience and intervening positively in their interaction, rather than allowing the loss of momentum and motivation that can arise under less favourable conditions.

The wider curriculum presents an even more important issue in continuity. The expansion of the informal curriculum is something that appeals at once: new games, new activities, new patterns of social relationships within these informal activities. In the school as a whole, which they always approach with some initial apprehension, they have to revert to being small fry, whereas in primary education they were the leaders in informal activities; but usually there are versions of informal education in their own class, or year, or tutor set which enable them to retain some confidence while they find their feet in the larger setting.

Alongside this can be found a rather more cautious response to the new organisational curriculum which at first appears bewildering, but which can itself provide an arena of criticism. The very fact that development is continuing makes it less likely that any secondary school organisation will be accepted even to the extent that primary schools are accepted. It becomes increasingly probable that messages of conflict as well as of compliance will be derived from school and applied to society. But for most new entrants to secondary education this is for the future, and the immediate response is to get abreast of the new and complex world in which they have to live.

It is in the hidden curriculum that newcomers to secondary

schools may find their principal surprise. Having been accustomed to a mixture of messages that include a caring equality on the one hand and a reward for achievement and compliance on the other, they may now find that the second of these elements is considerably strengthened. To it may be added a new dimension, that of the significance of public examinations. Primary school may have been viewed as a place where you have to go in order to learn. Secondary school may come to be seen as a place where you have to go in order to pass examinations, and secondary teachers as people whose subject-centred interests and teaching styles are for the most part designed for that purpose. Those who are not in this category, such as teachers of the arts, PE and RE, may appear for that very reason to be of lesser status. This may in its turn be offset by powerful denials and by a deliberate adoption of a caring pastoral approach, but it becomes evident where the real incentives and sanctions are to be found. And if this is true of the pupils as a whole, it is also true that some tend to find themselves in approved groups and others in suspect groups. This may itself be reflected in the organisational curriculum, expressed in terms of setting or streaming, with outcomes of the kind that have been traced and analysed by Ball (1982) and Turner (1982), and interpreted by Hargreaves (1982), whose sustained attempt to suggest ways of improving 'paracurriculum' constitutes an important contribution to the debate.

Within the English system, where the existence of middle schools has made some comparisons possible, there is little sign that the basic pattern of response to new styles in curriculum varies radically when the age of transfer is altered, except that occasionally one hears of children from 9-13 middle schools being more critical of their first encounters with subject-based teaching in their high schools than would have been likely if their transfer had taken place at 11. In selective schools there is no reason to suppose that the outcome is substantially different from what takes place in comprehensive schools, except that the contrast in content and teaching styles may be a little more marked. As for transfer between stages in independent schools, it appears likely to involve a quickening of pace in both formal and wider curriculum, rather than a fundamental contrast in approach or in pedagogy as may be the case in the public system.

Transition between schools in other Western systems is not dissimilar, though in many cases it is more formalised, so that the formal curriculum may well be more continuous from one stage to the next while the teaching styles and wider curriculum are more abruptly different. In the Soviet bloc much is made of entry to 'proper' school at the age of 7, but stages of transition within the main system do not appear to be specifically emphasised. But these are superficial generalisations: studies of transfer between stages have not hitherto been a major preoccupation of students of comparative education.

Thus, in one way or another, any system in which primary and secondary education are separated will embody some kind of transition that constitutes a rift in experience, and may send out shock waves into many other aspects of experience as new friends and new activities come into prominence, while others recede. It is a proof of enablement if this rift in experience is prepared for before it occurs, sympathetically understood when it occurs, and bridged by a change in curricular practice that is stimulating but not too abrupt.

### A Comparative Appraisal

Historically, the establishment of primary education itself has been associated with the way in which childhood has been defined (Sommerville, 1982). Obviously, in the simplest of pre-literate societies there has been no formal schooling, while children have always taken a positive part in family and economic activities in such societies as soon as they are physically able to do so. This last consideration emphasises that development must to some extent condition what children can do, but that is quite a different matter from setting aside a particular stage, or stages, of development for formal education in specific institutions located, in time-sequence, between family membership and adult status.

The introduction of a social institution specifically for boys or girls does not necessarily imply that it should be a school, or that there should be a formal curriculum. In some pre-literate societies there have been institutions for young people of specific age-levels, with secret codes and with rites of passage for entry and for completion, within which social skills including hunting and fighting have been learned in common under the guidance of elders in the society specifically chosen for this purpose. This social provision is clearly related to development, and involves tight control, so that this arrangement must be regarded as the equivalent of a formal curriculum, with wider implications, so comprehensive that it determines experience rather than building on it. Yet it cannot be designated as schooling.

Within Western societies the further step of introducing formal schooling was a long and complex process. During most of that process formal education, even at the primary level (more accurately, at the elementary level) was a minority experience. It is only in comparatively recent times that childhood and its education have come to be established for the vast majority of citizens, and more recently still, that childhood and its education have been separated from adolescence and its education. There is an important literature on the emergence of childhood as a distinctive phenomenon, including the work of Ariès (1962), Musgrove (1964) Stone (1977), Sommerville (1982), Gammage (1982) and more speculatively, de Mause (1974). It could be said that two kinds of separation have taken place since early modern times in the West. One is the separation of childhood, as distinct from infancy, from the world of adult competence and its setting into a period of protected preparation. The other is the separation of one kind of childhood from another on social-class lines. To say that childhood is a middle-class invention would be to bring the two kinds of separation into one formula of doubtful validity, but it is during the rise of the bourgeoisie that childhood has become, as Schnell (1979) puts it, a part of social reality. He also suggests that it was the bourgeoisie, which developed secondary education for itself, that first distinguished childhood from adolescence and primary education from secondary education as a part of social reality essential to its own self-improvement and subsequently essential to the rest of society as a common good, first historically for boys and then for girls too. It might be added that it was when the concept of 'secondary education for all' became accepted in Western society that a distinctive *primary* education, with its own curriculum, became possible for all.

Viewed from the standpoint of development, this emergent definition of childhood and of childhood education suggests that the categories of development operationally postulated in Chapter 1, and often taken for granted in discussions of primary education, need to be reconsidered. Physical development is relatively invariable as a category, though its pace may be subject to Tanner's (1961) 'secular trend'. Intellectual development is clearly more open to social influences, while social/emotional development is very largely particular to specific societies, as anthropologists are at pains to point out. So it is true to say that over the centuries the introduction of the concept of childhood and its education has done as much to determine development, as development has done to set constraints upon curriculum. This interaction over time introduces an important variable into the whole consideration of the relationship of curriculum to development.

Experience too figures differently when a substantial time-interval is considered. The range of experience, both in school and outside school, has increased immensely since, for example, the time when Pestalozzi sought self-realisation among the children of the poor in the Swiss cantons. It could even be said that schooling, which was introduced to widen experience, has reached a point when it finds difficulty in keeping pace with experience in the world outside. So when an enabling curriculum is defined as planned intervention in the interaction between development and experience, it becomes essential to place this in the context of a historical sequence in which both development and experience alter their valency from time to time, and in which the balance between the formal and wider curricula also alters. To make this assertion is to invite comment and criticism from Marxists and any others with a philosophy of history, especially when this implies also a standpoint for the present and the future.

It is indeed necessary next to consider the present and future context of primary education and to examine how far, in this respect, the social definition of childhood and of childhood education may in fact be changing, and what implications this change may have for the implementation of an enabling curriculum.

A world map of approaches to the primary curriculum would show, markedly, how far curricula of this kind are concentrated in the affluent West. It might bring out the current reality most clearly if the poorest societies are considered first. There, especially in those such as Burundi or Bangladesh, a situation exists which is not far removed from the pre-literate societies without formal educational institutions to which reference has already been made. Others with rather more material resources are not in much better situations. The basic fabric of primary education is sustained only patchily and with the help of outside agencies. Drop-outs are frequent (Levy, 1971), mainly because the economy of families and communities cannot afford to be deprived of child participation, but also because the quality of the teaching is so limited. The parallel with pre-industrial Europe in, say, the age of Comenius is evident.

Moreover, it is a commonplace dilemma of primary education in many territories in Africa and elsewhere that resources simply will not extend to the provision of adequate primary education for all (Heynemann and Loxley, 1983) until there has been enough secondary education to provide primary teachers, but that until adequate primary education for all has already been established, the economy is too fragile to be able to support the superstructure on which indigenous secondary education can be sustained (see, for example, Jennings-Wray, 1980)[1]. What is more, the grave nutritional and other impediments to development, and the severe limitation and tragedy of so much experience, make the language of Western curriculum development sound almost obscene when applied in this context. Yet it is necessary to come to terms with the ethical and moral issues involved in designing an enabling curriculum for declining numbers of children in California or Surrey or Bavaria, or even in Merseyside or Alabama or the Mezzogiorno, while the most that many of mankind's burgeoning children can be enabled to do is to survive and take part in elementary agriculture or herding or trading for a little while, before reaching adulthood and family responsibilities of their own.

There is, of course, a considerable part of the earth's surface in which life well beyond the subsistence level is possible at least for some of the population and their children. Yet here, in many cases, there are other major preoccupations that dwarf in practice the nostrums of curriculum planning. Prominent among these is the endeavour to establish national independence and political and social development: the 'political kingdom' which Kwame Nkrumah urged his people to 'seek first'. It is not surprising that in such societies, at the moment when it first becomes feasible to consider primary education beyond the barest minimum, it is the social-imperatives approach that predominates. Although some reflection of Western ideas on curriculum is to be found in some former colonial territories, the formal and informal curriculum is permeated with the official ideology, and great efforts are made to promote it. Ironically, the forms-of-understanding approach is often harnessed to the same ends, on the assumption that it will enable developing countries to take what is important from Western culture and adapt it, as Japan did, to lay the basis for their own prosperity and greatness. This applies not only to Western technology, for which the pure sciences are usually adopted, but also to Western literatures and other arts. The moral and religious forms of understanding are usually viewed with more suspicion as imports and, although indigenous churches and institutions of higher education may be encouraged, morality is quite likely to be subjected to whatever ideology is current at the time. For there are instances of the whole orientation of primary education being altered, through the issue of a new series of textbooks and syllabuses, when a new president is elected or when some ruling junta is re-shuffled. It must be added that a Marxist regime is less susceptible to this form of readjustment, though not entirely immune to it.

Among these societies there are some which exist in a state of almost permanent civil or foreign conflict: in the Middle East, in Indo-China, in the Sahara and in parts of Latin America. Here a different phenomenon also appears. For in addition to the officially imposed curricula of primary schooling imposed by governments or guerillas, there is enforced participation in the conflict itself. There is perhaps nothing that shocks the Western concept of childhood more than the incorporation of children, girls as well as boys, in actual fighting. It violates the ideology of childhood built up, as we have seen, during the past two or three centuries, and breaks down the accepted division between children and adults. For while grown men and women wail openly like their children over the ruins of their home and the bodies of their kin, the children throw their petrol bombs and carry firearms like their parents, and live for the day when they can become freedom fighters, of one sort or another, in their own right. In such circumstances development is cruelly accelerated, experience is tinged with some excitement, more devotion and much horror, and curriculum, in its separate world of school, almost vanishes from sight, or is itself made a symbolic target or recruiting ground, as on the West Bank of the Jordan. The boundary of primary education has been virtually overrun.

The third group of non-Western societies is that of the Communist bloc. Here, at least, primary education is more firmly established, and upheld by the might of the state. It has one point in common with the preceding group of societies, namely that the social-imperatives approach dominates the curriculum, yet also makes considerable use of forms of understanding. The pattern is similar, though not identical, throughout the huge Eurasian core of Marxist states and their more widely flung outliers. Pre-schooling, which is notably gentle and even indulgent yet ideologically inflexible, gives way at the age of 7 to the beginnings of the unified school, which has long since thrown off the memory of Dewey (once highly regarded in both the Soviet Union and China) and which now follows unapologetically a subject-based curriculum, flanked by a carefully planned informal, organisational and hidden curriculum that attempts to control all of life. Some gestures are made to development and to experience, especially in the wider curriculum with its close links with other social agencies such as the Octobrists and Young Pioneers, but there is little place for experience beyond the wider curriculum. As for the notion of a curriculum designed as planned intervention in the interaction between development and experience, that would be, in the phrase made familiar in diplomatic exchanges, 'utterly unacceptable'. The concept of enablement might well be endorsed as desirable, but it would have to enable the individual to become the citizen, and for that purpose there is only one agency, the Party (Bronfenbrenner, 1970).

It is thus not difficult to see that, in the present historical phase, an enabling curriculum of the nature described in the preceding chapters is virtually bound to be confined to the Western world: Western Europe, English-speaking North America, and Australasia. (South Africa cannot merit inclusion, nor can Israel, despite some features of its system). But even in these relatively well-to-do societies it is far from true to say that an enabling curriculum, developed from a process approach, is widely established and supported. On the contrary, it has been patchily developed even in bastions such as the United Kingdom, the USA, the Old Commonwealth, the Netherlands and Sweden, while in some Mediterranean countries it is almost unknown. There was indeed a brief and intriguing period, from about 1905 to 1925, when its momentum seemed irresistible. The 'progressive' movement (a term which has not been used systematically in the present discussion because of its overtones) then made a literally world-wide impact. Then one by one, different regimes opposed it: Fascist Italy, Nazi Germany and Stalin's USSR. After 1945 there was some revival of the 'progressive' ideology, but there is evidence that in more recent years it has been losing rather than gaining ground even in its Western stronghold. The attack upon progressivism, the seedbed of the process approach and of the kind of enabling curriculum advocated in the earlier discussion, has come from both Right and Left in the sociopolitical spectrum, and it is to this attack and its possible consequences for the future of an enabling curriculum, that we now have to turn.

The attack from the Right has not basically altered in character since the progressive movement began. The whole notion of a process approach, with consequent caution about forms of understanding and endeavour and even more so about social imperatives, has always been suspect to the upholders of tradition in Western societies. Recently, however, they have spoken with much more confidence. The cause of this increased confidence is twofold. On the one hand, the adoption of a process approach has been represented as softening the intellectual and moral fibre of nations. On the other, it has been blamed for industrial inefficiency and conflict. The consequences of this attack on the process approach from the Right have been felt increasingly in England since the Plowden Report (CACE, 1967), now often singled out as the apogee of progressivism. There has been increasing demand for accountability, which has in turn trimmed the opportunities for an enabling curriculum to be developed in schools, and this has become a characteristic of attitudes expressed not only on the Right but across the whole political spectrum of Western societies.

Especially since the mid-1960s the assumptions on which an enabling curriculum is based have come under fire also from the New Left. This the Right has perhaps been slow to recognise, for 'progressivism' as here discussed is often perceived by the Right as part of the same insidious and enervating corruption of education as they perceive more stridently in Marxism. Yet to the New Left, the kind of progressivism that flourished during and after the First World War can be seen as a means of reinforcing bourgeois individualism and of ignoring, or even deliberately contradicting, the realities of the class struggle. For one thing, the progressive approach, epitomised in England in the Plowden Report, proposes to enable middle-class as well as working-class children. For another, it intends to do so in terms of their individual development and experience rather than of a social analysis that claims to have scientific insight into what are their real needs and how they may be enabled to meet those needs. The burden of Sharp's and Green's (1975) analysis of infant-school teaching in the formal and wider curriculum is that the organisational and hidden aspects constitute, even if unconsciously, a means of preserving the social order while claiming to treat individuals in a child-centred equal fashion. It has been quoted extensively since, and criticised too, for example in the work of King (1978). It has, however, drawn attention to an important issue concerning the functions of primary education, and may contribute to the thinking of those who, following the thinking of

Gramsci (Entwistle, 1979), see in child-centred education an instrument by which the proletariat can be deprived of access to the forms of understanding necessary to the acquisition of economic and political power.

Thus, in England there is a genuine reaction against progressive and child-centred education, which has parallels elsewhere. Its extent can be exaggerated, just as the extent of child-centred education itself was exaggerated, on account of the visibility of its protagonists. Nevertheless, it must be taken into account in any sober estimation of the future potentialities of an enabling curriculum in primary education. Nor is this all. There are already signs that some of the characteristics of childhood outside the West are beginning to affect the internal balance and to tilt it more violently. In parts of Northern Ireland the 'militarisation' of childhood has gained some foothold in parts of both 'communities', as the presence of paramilitary organisations has become a conspicuous and pervasive part of experience. Already in the major conurbations in mainland Britain and in the USA, ethnic and other minorities have begun to manifest extremist organisations whose appeal to children of primary school age has something in common with that of the IRA or the PLO, and encourages the rejection of teachers as racists. Meanwhile, there are indications, in very recent times, that there may be forces on the Right in Western societies that, seeing those societies faced with subversion and unrest as well as with rising crime rates even among children between the ages of 5 and 10, begin to feel that the education of childhood is too important a matter to be left to schools and teachers.

## Conclusion

Where, then, does this leave the prospect for an enabling curriculum of the kind outlined in the previous chapters? Must it be regarded as nothing more than a temporary, fair-weather product of a short-lived, late-capitalist liberal experiment in a post-imperialist age, or even a piece of word-spinning lacking the test of praxis? These questions must be faced squarely if the enabling curriculum is to be seen as something more than just what it appears, in these criticisms, to be. In conclusion, a claim will be hazarded that an enabling curriculum is necessary for the maintenance of the best values embodied in Western society and for their refinement, and maybe as a component of primary education in other societies too.

That claim must be based on the principal features of this curriculum. First, it is grounded in development and in experience. Therefore, it is related to the social reality that each child knows and constructs. Other kinds of curricula are in some measure imposed, but in a society claiming to be democratic, curriculum must in some sense arise from the experience of children themselves.

Second, it goes beyond development and beyond experience. It is just where they interact that the curriculum intervenes, to encourage development and to widen experience. This is why it is to be viewed as an enabling curriculum. But its enabling arises in part from its readiness to confront children with reality, including the reality of different societies with different schools and different curricula.

Third, it is based on a process approach. This in itself, by emphasising the strengthening of skills and concepts and the beneficial change of attitudes, is a major aspect of enablement.

Fourth, it introduces children to the wider world through forms of understanding and endeavour. In this way it takes note both of the ways in which understanding has grown over the years, and of the propensity of children to learn in different modes.

Fifth, it deliberately avoids giving preference to any one set of social imperatives rather than another.

Sixth, it is concerned with both the formal and the wider curriculum, and does not try to confine education within subjects or even institutions.

In all of these ways, an enabling curriculum appears particularly well suited to a developing democracy. It is neither predetermined nor nebulous. It makes demands, certainly, on teachers, but it claims also the resources that they need for its implementation. Through its flexibility it caters for change in the social order; through its discipline it meets that change with determination and acceptance. For all of this it requires that a democratic society should entrust teachers with professional authority, and should be ready to support them even when schools become critical of society, on the grounds that, ultimately, society will benefit. For either the school will be wrong, in which case it will learn that it is wrong and, profit from the lesson; or society will be wrong, in which case the school will have corrected the perspective and encouraged a change for the better. In either case the children will be face to face with

## An Enabling Curriculum in Perspective 165

real issues and with the relevance of school. Other kinds of society would cavil at such trust, but may be prepared to allow some play for enabling education at some point in their structure, and it is likely that they will benefit in some measure in so far as they are able and willing to do so.

It could be said that these arguments for an enabling curriculum in primary education, if they are valid, must apply *a fortiori* to post-primary education. That would be the case if development and experience could be overlooked. Yet increasingly it appears that in secondary education an enabling curriculum may be swamped by the tendency for development and experience to contract out of school. Despite the vision and determination of many secondary school staffs, and of writers such as Hargreaves (1982), it appears that the primary years, extending perhaps to the age of 13, are those in which development and experience can be most readily influenced by curriculum. With the continuing fall in the age of physical and social maturity it begins to appear open to question whether compulsory secondary schooling will continue to be viable in its present form. Compulsion was introduced in Western (and other) societies as a means of securing equality of opportunity. For some it represents instead a means of community control over young people who might respond with much greater enthusiasm if they could finally discharge their obligation to be educated in a college rather than a school environment. The spectacle of so much conflict and frustration between teachers and pupils in the middle and upper parts of secondary schools is not a matter that can be viewed with complacency in Western societies.

If there were to be a general obligation for young people over 13 or 14 to decide where, and even when, to complete their formal education, the consequences for the education of younger children would be striking. Something like a middle school system would become necessary to cater for the highest age-groups within the compulsory structure, and something like a first school system for their juniors. A pre-school organisation might also be needed. Within this structure many of the values of an enabling curriculum could be carried forward to the end of what would then be compulsory schooling, as distinct from compulsory education. For it is in the primary years, in the broad sense, that an enabling curriculum can be seen to operate most effectively. Incidentally, within a flexible structure of this kind it would be easier to break down the boundaries between first and middle schools, including an extension of vertical grouping and intermediate-generation teaching as mentioned in Chapter 7, and also between primary schools and their communities.

The institution of a system on these lines would lead to a different pattern of change from what is often envisaged. For example, Oliver (1982) in his suggestions for planning the primary curriculum, sees particular value in a systematic forms-of-understanding approach which would thus lay a firm foundation for secondary education, but which would certainly not be bound to subjects in the primary years. This would meet the claims of continuity, and is demonstrably based on successful experience, but it is derived from a different set of assumptions about the nature of development and of experience. Blenkin and Kelly, in their valuable general study *The Primary Curriculum* (1981) prefer to advocate the upthrust of something like an enabling curriculum into the secondary school itself. This position is also supported at least in part by Gammage's *Children and Schooling* (1982) which also explores some of the historical and other issues relevant to curriculum for younger children. Both, however, expect that secondary education itself would retain its present function.

A characteristically radical suggestion has been made by Stonier (1982). Starting from the dramatic changes expected in technology and its social applications, he sketches a model of public education that assigns to secondary education many of the activities hitherto associated with further education, and also postulates that much of the future acquisition of basic skills and information will take place in the home and in small peer groups, with the consequence that primary education, not secondary education, would disappear. Stonier makes interesting references both to children teaching children and to the educational function of different kinds of adults, but the social function of primary education does not figure in his planning.

Thus, none of these recent writers actually envisages a situation in which primary education, rather than secondary education, remains central to the concerns of Western society, with common experience of schooling extending only to 13 or 14. It is easy to conjecture that this is because any modification of compulsion could so easily be converted into a new form of privileged or selective education. This need not, and should not, be the consequence. It would be quite possible for the range of necessary provision to be offered both in school and in college, for pupils over

14, or it might be preferable to transfer the whole process into a community college with adult status. In either case, an enabling curriculum in the extended primary years would constitute the basis on which a constructive sequel could be most effectively erected. To achieve this, in a Western democratic society, is a great deal. Beyond this are the value-questions that it raises, but cannot ultimately answer. That is as far as human enablement, through a secular institution, can go.

**Note**

(1) A recent issue of the *International Review of Education*, 29, 2 (1983) devoted to the topic 'The Universalization of Primary Education', explores these issues further.

# Appendix I

## An Enabling Curriculum for Primary Education

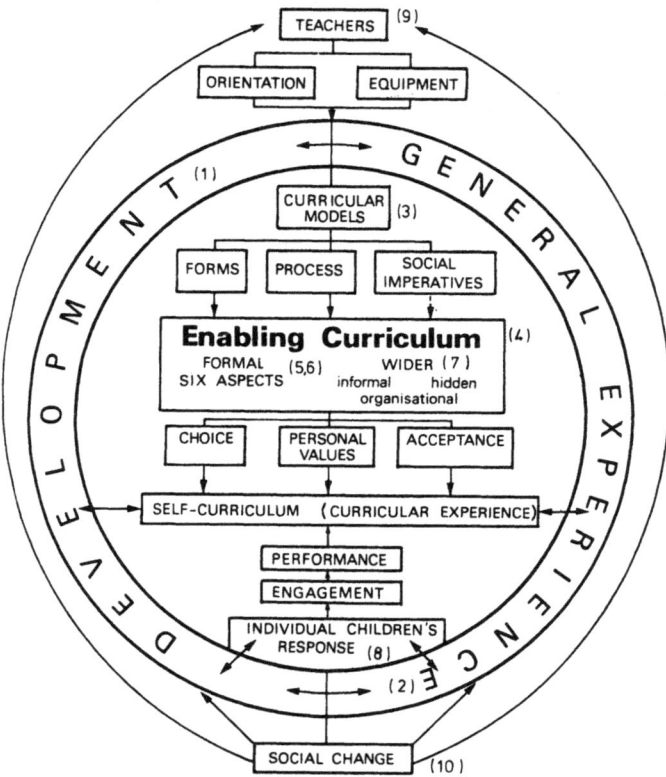

Chapter numbers in parentheses

# Appendix II

## Examples of Autobiography and Fiction Mentioned in Chapter 8

Ashley, Bernard *Terry on the Fence* (OUP, 1975, and Puffin, 1978)
Betjeman, John *Summoned by Bells* (John Murray, 1960)
Forrester, Helen *Twopence to Cross the Mersey* (Jonathan Cape, 1974)
——*Minerva's Stepchild* (Bodley Head, 1979)
Both of these volumes are now re-issued by Fontana Books, the latter under the title *Liverpool Lass*, together with the last part of the trilogy, *By the Waters of Liverpool*
Gardam, Jane *A Long Way from Verona* (Hamish Hamilton, 1971)
Kemp, Gene *The Turbulent Term of Tyke Tiler* (Faber & Faber, 1977, and Puffin, 1979)
——*Gowie Corby Plays Chicken* (Faber and Faber, 1979, and Puffin, 1981)
Lively, Penelope *Going Back* (Heinemann, 1975, and Pan Books, 1977)
Needle, Jan *My Mate Shofiq* (Andre Deutsch, 1978)
Toynbee, Philip *A School in Private* (Putnam, 1941)
Wakefield, Tom *Forties Child* (Routledge & Kegan Paul, 1980)

# BIBLIOGRAPHY

Adamson, J.W. *The Educational Writings of John Locke* (Cambridge UP, 1922)
Alexander, R.J. *Primary Teaching: Practice, Justification and Professional Context* (Holt Saunders, forthcoming)
Allen, V.L. *Children as Teachers: Theory and Research on Tutoring* (New York, Academic Press, 1976)
Alston, Philomena, M. *An Exploratory Study of Some Cognitive Aspects of Musical Proficiency* (Thesis for degree of Ph D, University of Liverpool, 2 vols, 1979)
Ariès, P. *Centuries of Childhood* (New York, Random House, 1962)
Armstrong, M. *Closely Observed Children* (Writers and Readers Co-operative and Chameleon Press, 1981)
Arnold, P. *Meaning in Movement, Sport and Physical Education* (Heinemann, 1979)
Ashton, P.M. et al. *The Aims of Primary Education : A Study of Teachers' Opinions* (Macmillan Education, 1975)
——'Primary Teachers' Approaches to Personal and Social Behaviour' in B. Simon and J. Willcocks (eds), *Research and Practice in the Primary Classroom* (Routledge & Kegan Paul, 1981)
——et al. *Teacher Education in the Classroom* (Croom Helm, 1982)
Ball, S.J. *Beachside Comprehensive* (Cambridge UP, 1982)
Bantock, G.H. *Studies in the History of Educational Theory, I – Artifice and Nature, 1350–1765* (Allen & Unwin, 1980)
Barker Lunn, J. *Streaming in the Primary School: a Longitudinal Study of Children in Streamed and Non-streamed Junior Schools* (NFER, 1970)
Barnes, D. *From Communication to Curriculum* (Penguin, 1976)
Bassey, M. *Nine Hundred Primary Teachers* (Slough, NFER, 1978)
Bennett, S.N. *Teaching Styles and Pupil Progress* (Open Books, 1976)
——et al. *Open Plan Schools: Teaching, Curriculum, Design* (NFER for Schools Council, 1980)
Bernstein, B. *Class, Codes and Control—3—Towards a Theory of Educational Transmissions* (Routledge & Kegan Paul, 1975)
Blenkin, G. and Kelly, A.V. *The Primary Curriculum* (Harper & Row, 1981)
——(eds) *The Primary Curriculum in Action: a Process Approach to Educational Practice* (Harper & Row, 1983)
Blyth, W.A.L. *English Primary Education: a Sociological Description*, 2 vols (Routledge & Kegan Paul, 1965)
——and Derricott, R. *The Social Significance of Middle Schools* (Batsford, 1977)
Bloom, B.S., Krathwohl, D.R. et al. *Taxonomy of Educational Objectives*, 2 vols, (Longmans, 1956, 1964)
Boardman, D. *Graphicacy and Geography Teaching* (Croom Helm, 1983)
Bossert, S.T. *Tasks and Social Relationships in Classrooms: a Study of Instructional Organisation and its Consequences* (Cambridge UP, 1979)
Bronfenbrenner, U. *Two Worlds of Childhood: U.S. and USSR* (New York, Russell Sage Foundation, 1970)
Brown, C. and Turnock, J. 'Curriculum Design in the Two/Three Teacher School', *Curriculum* 2.2, 28–34, 1981
Bruner, J.S. *The Process of Education* (Cambridge, Mass., Harvard University Press, 1960)
——*Towards a Theory of Instruction* (Cambridge, Mass., Belknap Press, 1966)
Bryan, K.A. 'Pupil Perceptions of Transfer Between Middle and High Schools', in A. Hargreaves and L. Tickle, (eds) *Middle Schools: Origins, Ideology and*

*Practice* (Harper & Row, 1980)
CACE (Central Advisory Council for Education (England)) *Children and Their Primary Schools* (Plowden Report) 2 vols, (HMSO, 1967)
Calvert, B. *The Role of the Pupil* (Routledge & Kegan Paul, 1975)
Clarricoats, K. 'The Importance of Being Ernest . . . Emma . . . Tom . . . Jane', in R. Deem (ed.) *Schooling for Women's Work* (Routledge & Kegan Paul, 1980)
Clift, P.S., Weiner, G. and Wilson, E. *Record-keeping in Primary Schools* (Schools Council Research Series, Macmillan Education, 1981)
Cobb, E. *The Ecology of Imagination in Childhood* (Routledge & Kegan Paul, 1977)
Consultative Committee of the Board of Education, *Report on the Primary School* (Haslow Report) (HMSO, 1931)
Cooper, K.R. *Evaluation, Assessment and Record-keeping in History, Geography and Social Science*, Schools Council Project, *History, Geography and Social Science 8 – 13* (Collins/ESL, Bristol, 1976)
Croall, J. *Neill of Summerhill* (Routledge & Kegan Paul, 1983)
Curtis, B. and Mays, W. (eds) *Phenomenology and Education* (Methuen, 1978)
Davey, A.G. and Mullin, P.N. 'Inter-ethnic Friendship in British Primary Schools', *Educational Research*, 24,2, pp. 83-92 (1982)
Davies, B. *Life in the Classroom and Playground: the Accounts of Primary School Children* (Routledge & Kegan Paul, 1982)
Dean, J. *Religious Education for Children* (Ward Lock Educational, 1971)
——*Organising Children's Learning in the Primary School Classroom* (Croom Helm, 1983)
Dearden, R.F. *The Philosophy of Primary Education* (Routledge & Kegan Paul, 1968)
De Mause, L. *The History of Childhood* (New York, Psychohistory, 1974)
DES (Department of Education and Science (England and Wales)) *Curriculum 11 – 16: Working Papers by HM Inspectorate: a Contribution to the Current Debate*, (HMSO, 1977)
——*Primary Education in England: A Survey by HM Inspectors of Schools* (HMSO, 1978)
Dewey, J. *Experience and Education* (New York, Kappa Delta Pi, 1938; New York, Collier-Macmillan 1963)
——*Democracy and Education* (New York, Macmillan, 1916; New York, Free Press 1966)
Donaldson, M. *Children's Minds* (Fontana/Collins, 1978)
Duska, R. and Whelan, M. *Moral Development: a Guide to Piaget and Kohlberg* (Dublin, Gill & Macmillan, 1977)
Egan, K. *Educational Development* (Oxford UP, 1979)
Eisner, E.H. *Educating Artistic Vision* (New York, Macmillan, 1972)
Eggleston, S.J. *The Sociology of the School Curriculum* (Routledge & Kegan Paul, 1977)
Ennever, L.F. et al. *With Objectives in Mind: Guide to Science 5–13*, Schools Council Project, *Science 5–13* (Macdonald Educational, 1972)
Entwistle, H. *Antonio Gramsci* (Routledge & Kegan Paul, 1979)
Erikson, E.H. *Childhood and Society* (New York, W.W. Norton, Inc., 1950; Penguin Books, 1965 and reprints)
Fleming, C.M. *Research and the Basic Curriculum* (University of London Press, 1946)
Galton, M., Simon, B. and Croll, P. (eds) *Inside the Primary Classroom* (Routledge & Kegan Paul, 1980a)
——and Simon, B. (eds) *Progress and Performance in the Primary Classroom* (Routledge & Kegan Paul, 1980b)
——and Willcocks, J. (eds) *Moving From the Primary Classroom* (Routledge &

Kegan Paul, 1983)
Gammage, P. *Children and Schooling* (Allen & Unwin, 1982)
Garforth, F.W. *Locke's Thoughts Concerning Education* (Heinemann, 1964)
—— *John Locke's On the Conduct of the Understanding* (New York, Teachers College, 1966)
Gentle, K. 'The Development of Children's Art', *Education 3–13*, 9,2,20-4 (1981)
—— *Teaching Art 5–13* (Croom Helm, 1983)
Gesell, A. *Studies in Child Development* (New York and London, Harper, 1948)
Grace, G.R. *Role Conflict and the Teacher* (Routledge & Kegan Paul, 1972)
Hargreaves, A. and Tickle, L. (eds) *Middle Schools: Origins, Ideology and Practice* (Harper & Row, 1980)
Hargreaves, D.H. 'Power and the Paracurriculum', in C. Richards *Power and the Curriculum: Issues in Curriculum Studies* (Driffield, Nafferton Books, 1978)
—— *The Challenge of the Comprehensive School: Culture, Curriculum and Community* (Routledge & Kegan Paul, 1982)
Harlen, W. *Match and Mismatch. 1. Raising Questions. 2. Finding Answers* (Oliver & Boyd, for the Schools Council, 1977)
Havighurst, R.J. *Human Development and Education* (Longmans, 1953)
Heynemann, S.P. and Loxley, W.A. 'The Distribution of Primary School Quality Within High- and Low-income Countries', *Comp. Educ. Rev.*, 27,1,108-18 (1983)
Hoyle, E. *The Role of the Teacher* (Routledge & Kegan Paul, 1969)
Hutchcroft, D.M.R. *Making Language Work* (McGraw Hill, 1981)
Isaacs, S. *Childhood and After: Some Essays and Clinical Studies* (Routledge, 1948)
Jackson, P.W. *Life in Classrooms* (New York, Rinehart & Winston, 1968)
Jennings-Wray, Z.D. 'A Comparative Study of Influences and Constraints on Decision-making in the Primary School Curriculum: Some Implications for Teachers as an Agent of Change in Third World Countries', *J. Curric. Studies*, 12,3,231-44 (1980)
Johnston, D. 'Curriculum Change and Research in a Middle School', in B. Simon and J. Willcocks (eds), *Research and Practice in the Primary Classroom* (Routledge & Kegan Paul, 1981)
Kelly, A.V. 'Research and the Primary Curriculum', *J. Curric. Studies*, 13,3, 215-25 (1981)
—— *The Curriculum: Theory and Practice*, 2nd edn (Harper & Row, 1982)
King, R. *All Things Bright and Beautiful: a Sociological Study of Infants' Classrooms* (Routledge & Kegan Paul, 1978)
Kirby, N. *Personal Values in Primary Education* (Harper & Row, 1981)
Kohlberg, L. and Mayer R. 'Development as the Aim of Education', *Harvard Educational Review*, 42,4, 449-96 (1972)
Laban, R. *Modern Educational Dance* (Macdonald and Evans, 1948)
Lawton, D. et al. *Social Studies 8–13*, Schools Council Working Paper No. 39. (Evans/Methuen Educational, 1971)
Levy, M.B. 'Determinants of Primary School Dropouts in Developing Countries', *Comp. Educ. Rev.*, 15,1, 44-58 (1971)
Lowenfeld, V. and Brittain, W.L. *Creative and Mental Growth*, 7th edn (New York, Macmillan, 1982)
Maslow, A. *Motivation and Personality* (New York, Harper & Row, 1954)
McPhail, P. et al. *Moral Education in the Middle Years* (Startline) (Longmans, for the Schools Council, 1978)
—— *Social and Moral Education* (Blackwell, 1982)
Meyenn, R.L. 'Peer Networks among Middle School Pupils', in A. Hargreaves and L. Tickle (eds), *Middle Schools: Origins, Ideology and Practice* (Harper & Row, 1980)

Midwinter, E.C. *Education and the Community* (Unwin Education, 1975)
Moore, R. *Childhood's Domain: Play and Place in Child Development* (Croom Helm, 1984)
Musgrove, F. *Youth and the Social Order* (Routledge & Kegan Paul, 1964)
——and Taylor, P.H. *Society and the Teacher's Role* (Routledge & Kegan Paul, 1969)
Nash, R. *Classrooms Observed: the Teacher's Perception and the Pupil's Performance* (Routledge & Kegan Paul, 1973)
Nicholls, A. and H. *Developing a Curriculum: a Practical Guide* (Unwin Education, 1972)
Oakeshott, M. *Experience and its Modes* (Cambridge UP, 1933)
Oliver, D. 'The Primary Curriculum: a Proper Basis for Planning', in C. Richards (ed.), *New Directions in Primary Education* (Falmer Press, 1982)
Oswin, M. *Children Living in Long-Stay Hospitals* (Heinemann Medical, 1978)
Paisey, A. *Small Organisations: the Management of Primary and Middle Schools* (NFER/Nelson, 1981)
Peters, R.S. (ed.), *Perspectives on Plowden* (Routledge & Kegan Paul, 1969)
Piaget, J. *The Moral Judgement of the Child*, tr. M. Gabain (Routledge & Kegan Paul, 1932)
Pluckrose, H. *Let's Use the Locality* (Mills & Boon, 1971)
Richards, C.M. *New Directions in Primary Education* (Falmer Press, 1982)
Ridgway, L. and Lawton, I. *Family Grouping in the Primary School* (Ward Lock Educational, 1968)
Riesman, D. *The Lonely Crowd* (New Haven, Conn., Yale University Press, 1956)
Ross, A.M. et al. *The Curriculum in the Middle Years*, Schools Council Working Paper No. 55. (Evans/Methuen Educational, 1975)
Schnell, R.L. 'Childhood as Ideology: a Reinterpretation of the Common School', *Brit. J. Educ. Studies*, XXVII, 1,7-28 (1979)
Sharp, R. and Green, A. *Education and Social Control: A Study in Progressive Primary Education* (Routledge & Kegan Paul, 1975)
Shipman, M.D. *Assessment in Primary and Middle Schools* (Croom Helm, 1983)
Simon, B. and Willcocks, J. (eds) *Research and Practice in the Primary Classroom* (Routledge & Kegan Paul, 1981)
Sluckin, A. *Growing Up in the Playground: the Social Development of Children* (Routledge & Kegan Paul, 1981)
Sommerville, C.J. *The Rise and Fall of Childhood* (Beverley Hills, Sage Publications, 1982)
Southgate, V. et al. *Extending Beginning Reading* (Heinemann Educational, for the Schools Council, 1981)
Staines, J.W. 'Perspectives and Values in Education for Self-discovery' in J.B. Annand (ed.), *Education for Self-discovery* (Hodder & Stoughton, 1977)
Steel, D.J. and Taylor, L. *Family History in Schools* (Phillimore, 1973)
Steiner, R. *Education as a Social Problem* (New York, Anthroposophical Press, Inc. 1969 (originally published 1919))
Stenhouse, L. *An Introduction to Curriculum Research and Development* (Heinemann, 1975)
——'Curriculum Research and the Art of the Teacher', *Curriculum*, 1,1,40-4 (1980)
Stevens, O. *Children Talking Politics* (Martin Robertson, 1982)
Stonier, T. 'Changes in Western Society: Educational Implications', in C. Richards (ed.), *New Directions in Primary Education* (Falmer Press, 1982)
Stone, L. *The Family, Sex and Marriage in England, 1500–1800* (Weidenfeld & Nicholson, 1977)
Stones, E. *Psychopedagogy* (Methuen, 1979)
Sutherland, M.B. *Everyday Imagining and Education* (Routledge & Kegan Paul,

1971)
Taba, H. *Curriculum Development: Theory and Practice* (New York, Harcourt, Brace & World, 1962)
Tanner, J.M. *Education and Physical Growth* (University of London Press, 1961)
Taylor, P.H. *et al. Purpose, Power and Constraint in the Primary School Curriculum* (Macmillan Education, 1974)
Thomas, D.J. *The Experience of Handicap* (Methuen, 1982)
Tough, Y.J. *The Development of Meaning* (Unwin Education, 1977a)
——'Talking and Learning: a Guide to the Fostering of Communication Skills', Schools Council Project, *Communication Skills in Early Childhood* (Ward Lock Educational, 1977b)
——'Talk for Teaching and Learning', Schools Council Project: *Communication Skills 7–13* (Ward Lock Educational, 1979)
Turner, G. *The Social World of the Comprehensive School* (Croom Helm, 1982)
Tyler, R.W. *Basic Principles of Curriculum and Instruction* (Chicago, University of Chicago Press, 1949)
UCET (Universities Council for the Education of Teachers) *Postgraduate Certificate in Education Courses for Teachers in Primary and Middle Schools* (UCET, 1982)
Vygotsky, L.S. *Thought and Language* (Boston, MIT Press, 1962)
Ward, C. and Fyson, A. *Streetwork: the Exploding School* (Routledge & Kegan Paul, 1973)
Wartella, E. (ed.) *Children Communicating: Media and Development of Thought, Speech, Understanding* (Beverley Hills, Sage Publications, 1979)
Watts, D.G. *Environmental Studies* (Routledge & Kegan Paul, 1969)
Whitehead, A.N. *The Aims of Education and Other Essays* (Williams & Norgate, 1932; also Ernest Benn, 1950 and reprints)
Wilson, P.S. *Interest and Discipline in Education* (Routledge & Kegan Paul, 1971)
Woods, P. and Hammersley, M. (eds), *School Experience* (Croom Helm, 1977)
Youngman, M.B. 'Six Reactions to School Transfer', *Brit. J. Educ. Psychol.*, 48,3, 280-9 (1978)

# INDEX

age-range: of primary education 152–3
Alexander, R.J. 1, 134
appreciation 67–71
armed conflict: and primary education 160; in Northern Ireland 163
Ashton, P.M. 27, 29, 138, 149
assessment: in an enabling curriculum 123, 135, 140–1, 150
attitudes: and formal curriculum 71–7; in relation to social understanding 89–90; in relation to wider curriculum 116–17

Bantock, G.H. 8
Bassey, M. 138
Bennett, S.N. 137–8
Berg, L. 66
Bernstein, B. 27, 31, 57, 148
Blenkin, G.A. 30, 51, 58, 166
Blyth, W.A.L. 106–7, 141; and Derricott, R. 142
Boardman, D. 80, 93
Bronfenbrenner, U. 108, 161
Bruner, J.S. 4, 23, 36, 60, 78, 84, 108; and spiral curriculum 84, 94, 100
Buddhist approach 76

child development 1
childhood, as culture phase 8, 156–8
children's response: to formal curriculum 121–4; to wider curriculum 124–6
children with special needs: response to curriculum 128–9
Christian approach 42, 74, 105, 115
Comenius, J.A. 8, 158
communication: and formal curriculum 56–9; and wider curriculum 113–14
curriculum, theories of: and curriculum processes 34–9, 84–6, 93–7; forms of understanding and experience 28–30, 34, 47; process 30–1, 34, 47–8, 93; social-imperatives 31–4, 45–7, 159

Dearden, R.F. 18, 36, 75
developmental theories of primary education 7–12
Dewey, J. 22, 42, 60, 63, 65, 73–4, 106, 143, 160–1
Donaldson, M. 3, 61
Durkheim, E. 23, 31, 74, 106

Egan, K. 11–12, 51
Eggleston, S.J. 29–30
enabling curriculum: basis 42–5, 49–50; definition 48–9; comparative context 156–61; implications for school system 165–6; opposition 51–2, 161–3; prospects 163–6
engagement, in response to curriculum 118–27
experience: Chapter 2 *passim*; meaning and characteristics 14–15, 18–20; outside curriculum 24, 112, 126–7; relation to development 15–17
experiential theories of primary education 20–5
expression, in curriculum 67–71

feeling, in curriculum 67–71
Froebel, F.W.A. 9–11, 63, 65, 68
Freud, S. 6, 10, 63

Galton, M.J. *see* ORACLE Project
Gammage, P. 157, 166
Goldman, R. 76
Gramsci, A. 32, 163
graphicacy 59, 80, 93
grouping in schools 107–9; in relation to formal curriculum 53–6; in relation to wider curriculum 112–13

Hadow Report (The Primary School) 32
Hargreaves, D.H. 155, 165
Havighurst, R.J. 6, 19
Health: in relation to formal curriculum 53–6; in relation to wider curriculum 112–13
Herbart, J.F. 21–3, 60, 74
hidden curriculum 100, 109–12

imagination: in relation to formal curriculum 63–7; in relation to wider curriculum 115
industry in primary education 92
informal curriculum 100–3
intellectual development 3–5, 82, 157; relation to social understanding 87–8
interests, relation to social understanding 89
interpretation of the world 59–63; curriculum planning 84–6, 93–7; social aspects, Chapter 6 *passim*; wider curriculum 114–15
Islamic approach 32, 74, 76, 105, 115

Judaic approach 105, 115

Kant, I. 21
Kelly, A.V. 30–1, 51, 58, 166
King, R. 137, 162
Kirby, N. 51
Kohlberg, L. 6, 72, 74–5, 104, 106; and Meyer, R. 12, 33

locality, local environment: in relation to social understanding 91
Locke, J. 20
Lowenfeld, V. 68–9

Marxist approach 7, 32, 37, 64, 74, 115, 158, 160–2
minorities in response to curriculum 127–32; ethnic 129–31
Midwinter, E.C. 33
Montessori, M. 10–11, 42, 63
moral education in an enabling curriculum 72–6
movement: in relation to formal curriculum 53–6; in relation to wider curriculum 112–13
multicultural education 92

Neill, A.S. 10

Oliver, D. 166
ORACLE Project 114, 118, 137–8, 153
organisational curriculum 100, 104–9

parental participation in curriculum 145
performance, in response to curriculum 118–27
personality development 5, 82, 157

Pestalozzi, J.H. 9, 21, 55, 158
Peters, R.S. 1, 12
physical development 2–3, 81, 157
Piaget, J. 4–6, 60–1, 72, 104, 106
Plowden Report 31, 152, 162
*Primary Education in England* Survey 59, 142
professional status-inversion 142, 147
project (method) 36–7

religious education in an enabling curriculum 76–7
research on an enabling curriculum 150–1
'responsible process approach' 93
Richards, C.M. 33, 51
Riesman, D. 73
Rousseau, J-J. 8–9, 21
rules, school 104–6

school-based curriculum innovation 142–4
Schools Council Projects: Health Education 5–13 56; Moral Education 8–13 74; Place, Time and Society 8–13 Chapter 6 *passim*; Science 5/13 62–3
self-curriculum 78, 109, 118–19, 121
sex education 54–6; roles 83
sexual development 2, 6
Sharp, R. and Green, A. 137, 162
Sluckin, A. 104, 111, 126
social development 5, 82, 157; relation to social understanding 88–9
Soviet schools 108, 160–1
Steiner, R. 10
Stenhouse, L. 35, 141–2
stereotypes 110–11, 129
Stones, E. 136
Stonier, T. 166
support agencies for curriculum innovation 144–8
Sutherland, M.B. 64

Taba, H. 36
Tanner, J.M. 2–3, 157
teacher education: initial, and an enabling curriculum 148–9; in-service, and an enabling curriculum 147–8
teachers: as researchers 141; development in 134; equipment required to enact an enabling curriculum 136–9; experience in 134–6; new roles 141–2, 146;

suitability to enact an enabling curriculum 136–9
Third World, primary education in 158–60
transition from primary education 153–6

unitary curriculum 77–8

values: in relation to formal curriculum 71–7; in relation to wider curriculum 116–17
vision: in relation to formal curriculum 63–7; in relation to wider curriculum 115

Whitehead, A.N. 4, 11

For Product Safety Concerns and Information please contact our EU representative GPSR@taylorandfrancis.com
Taylor & Francis Verlag GmbH, Kaufingerstraße 24, 80331 München, Germany

www.ingramcontent.com/pod-product-compliance
Lightning Source LLC
Chambersburg PA
CBHW051645230426
43669CB00013B/2449